sing with all the people of god

A HANDBOOK FOR CHURCH MUSICIANS

Chad Fothergill

Augsburg Fortress

SING WITH ALL THE PEOPLE OF GOD
A Handbook for Church Musicians

Also available:
Leading Worship Matters: A Sourcebook for Preparing Worship Leaders
    (ISBN 978-1-4514-7806-8)
Proclaiming the Living Word: A Handbook for Preachers (ISBN 978-1-5064-4789-6)
Embodying Confidence and Grace: A Handbook for Presiding Ministers
    (ISBN 978-1-5064-6076-5)
Praying for the Whole World: A Handbook for Intercessors (ISBN 978-1-5064-1596-3)
Serving the Assembly's Worship: A Handbook for Assisting Ministers (ISBN 978-1-4514-7808-2)
Getting the Word Out: A Handbook for Readers (ISBN 978-1-4514-7807-5)
Altar Guild and Sacristy Handbook, 4th rev. ed. (ISBN 978-1-4514-7809-9)
Worship Matters: An Introduction to Worship (Participant book ISBN 978-1-4514-3605-1;
    Leader guide ISBN 978-1-4514-3604-4)

Scripture quotations, unless otherwise noted, are from the New Revised Standard Version
Bible, © 1989 Division of Christian Education of the National Council of Churches of Christ
in the United States of America. Used by permission. All rights reserved.

Psalm translations from *Evangelical Lutheran Worship*, © 2006 Evangelical Lutheran Church
in America, admin. Augsburg Fortress.

Page 8 and page 84: "God, whose giving knows no ending," text © 1961, ren. 1989 The Hymn
Society, admin. Hope Publishing Company. Carol Stream, IL 60188. All rights reserved. Used
by permission.
Page 126: "Come to us, creative Spirit," text © 1979 Stainer & Bell Ltd., admin. Hope
Publishing Company. Carol Stream, IL 60188. All rights reserved. Used by permission.

Cover design: Lauren Williamson
Cover image: *Celebration* © 2019 John August Swanson | Eyekons
Interior design: Kristin Miller
Editor: Jennifer Baker-Trinity

Manufactured in the U.S.A.

ISBN 978-1-5064-6923-2
eISBN 978-1-5064-6956-0

24   23   22   21   20   1   2   3   4   5

Contents

Acknowledgments

Just as assembly song needs poets, translators, composers, editors, musicians, and an assembly to craft and assemble it, a book—even a petite book such as this—also requires many hands to steward it into being. I am grateful to Jennifer Baker-Trinity for the invitation to think more deeply about the vocation of church musicians, and to the staff of Augsburg Fortress and 1517 Media—editors, typesetters, proofreaders, artists, printers, and more—for the artistry, care, and patience required to transform a messy manuscript into the book you now hold.

Parts of this book are distillations and reworkings of previous writings that have appeared in *CrossAccent* and *In Tempo*, the two journals of the Association of Lutheran Church Musicians (ALCM), as well as in *Sundays and Seasons*, *Living Lutheran*, the *Prelude Music Planner* blog, and the *Reformation 500 Sourcebook*. The editors and publishers of these resources are acknowledged for permission to revisit these ideas, and appreciation is extended to ALCM, the Delaware Chapter of the American Guild of Organists, the Society for Christian Scholarship in Music, the Vi Messerli Memorial Lectures in Church Music at Concordia University Chicago, and the National Worship Conference of the Evangelical Lutheran and Anglican churches in Canada for opportunities provided to think, write, and speak about the church, its music, and its musicians.

Nor could this book have been possible without knowledge and skills imparted by scholars, pastors, mentors, hymn writers, fellow church musicians, choir members, students at Gustavus Adolphus College and the Lutheran Summer Music Academy and Festival, and members of congregations I have served in full-time, part-time, interim, and supply capacities. Their presence is reflected through fragments of hymn stanzas and morsels of wisdom that, through repetition and reflection, have seeped into my bones and, as a result, onto these pages. This is more theirs and your book than it is mine.

Birmingham, Alabama
Holy Cross Day
14 September 2019

"

Skills and time are ours for pressing
toward the goals of Christ, your Son:
all at peace in health and freedom,
races joined, the church made one.
Now direct our daily labor,
lest we strive for self alone;
born with talents, make us servants
fit to answer at your throne.

"God, whose giving knows no ending"
Evangelical Lutheran Worship, #678

Prelude

It is a Sunday morning in January, the festival of the Baptism of Our Lord. In the rural Midwest, a pianist has braved a long drive in subzero temperatures to accompany spirituals such as "Wade in the water" (ELW 459) chosen for the morning's liturgy. In the rainy Mid-Atlantic, a singer warms up the choir by teaching a newly composed, paperless acclamation to be sung during the thanksgiving for baptism. In the Southwest, a volunteer organist adjusts registrations for a Baroque chorale prelude based on Luther's baptism hymn "To Jordan came the Christ, our Lord" (LBW 79). In a large city near the Gulf Coast, a guitarist—who also happens to be a rostered deacon—checks over lead sheets to make sure that every member of the ensemble has their songs and hymns in the correct order. And in many other places and in various ways, church musicians set about their most important and fulfilling task: leading their respective assemblies in song.

The stylistic variety of these brief scenarios—not to mention the array of gifts, training, and experiences represented by these four musicians—reflects a small fraction of the diverse communities, spaces, and pieties in which church musicians serve. Each and every time the church gathers for worship, a dazzling abundance of musical expressions are voiced. Each time the people of God sing, a miraculous machine—a corporeal, cosmic symphony—is set in motion; a rhythmic pulse first felt in the song leader's body is, through articulation and steady timekeeping, given over to the assembly to take as its own. Within nanoseconds, an intricate system of nerves, neurons, and muscles transforms inked letterforms and symbols for musical notation on a printed page—perhaps from the same book held by someone down the street or across the country—into embodied sound. Or perhaps we bypass the page and, instead, sing by heart.

Whether singing a cappella or with accompaniment, many voices become one voice—breathing together, feeling a pulse together, sensing the arc of a melody and trajectory of a harmonic progression as one. Together these voices sing texts: psalms, hymns, and spiritual songs from poets of many times and places. Old words such as *Kyrie* or *Gloria* are sung to new melodies; new words are sung to old melodies. Regardless of style or accompaniment, bodies are synchronized. Diaphragms and rib cages move. Lungs are filled with breath. Lips, teeth, and tongues form vowels and consonants. All to sing Spirit-inspired texts that form, call, shape, and teach us to be the body of Christ in the world. Maybe there's some spittle, missed words, or wrong notes along the way. But that's okay; this is proclamation, praise, and prayer—not performance. It has been created by God, and it is good.

The singing of God's people—the songs themselves and ways in which they are selected and voiced in the assembly—is the principal subject of this handbook. Though written for those who primarily serve the church as musicians, hopefully its contents find use among pastors, worship committees, musician search committees, and all who join their voices in the hymn of all creation. Before proceeding to the chapters themselves, a few words about what this book is, what it isn't, some assumptions (perhaps presumptions) that it makes, and how it may be used.

The church musician's role is vocational

In sermons and other writings, Martin Luther was careful to distinguish between one's occupation (job) and one's vocation (calling). For Luther, vocation was oriented toward others, using God-given abilities in all aspects of daily life, whether at work, at home, in the community, or in the church. Vocation was not, as the word is sometimes used today, simply a trade or skill, but a response to God's call enacted on behalf of the wider community. As Mark Tranvik reminds us in *Martin Luther and the Called Life*, the Bible tells us that "God summons Moses so that he might lead the people of Israel out of bondage. Mary is called so that she might bear the one who fulfills God's promises to Israel and the world. The disciples are called so that they might constitute the beginnings of a new community charged with telling the world of a new way that God has acted in the person of Jesus of Nazareth."[1]

---

1   Mark D. Tranvik, *Martin Luther and the Called Life* (Minneapolis: Fortress Press, 2016), 22.

Like Moses, Mary, and the disciples, we are also called to vocations that serve God's people in many and various ways. Or, as one of the hymns in the Vocation, Ministry section of *Evangelical Lutheran Worship* teaches us:

> We all are one in mission,
> we all are one in call,
> our varied gifts united
> by Christ, the Lord of all.[2]

The concept of vocation has been important for Lutheran church musicians since the Reformation. In a large, three-volume biblical commentary that he owned, Johann Sebastian Bach marked passages about those who offer the first fruits of their God-given gifts on behalf of the nations and peoples, both in the church and in the city. Like their musical forebears, today's church musicians exercise their vocations in ways that transcend boundaries between work, home, community, and church. Through music, they share in the joys and sorrows of choir members and the assembly, watch God's children begin and end their baptismal journeys, and reveal profound scriptural and interpretive insights through their musical selections and leadership, both in worship and beyond. Their vocation is simultaneously musical, theological, and pastoral.

In our business-oriented, transactional, and individualistic culture, the concept of vocation is often given short shrift, if not

2   Rusty Edwards, "We all are one in mission," in *Evangelical Lutheran Worship*, #576.

entirely overlooked. Unfortunately the church is not immune to this way of thinking. Hierarchies sometimes replace partnerships, satisfaction surveys and employee evaluations are substituted for discernment, charisma trumps calling, and the desire to be relevant or authentic can easily displace the central importance of word and sacrament. At its worst, an occupational orientation is only concerned with musical products that church musicians can dispense: they, in effect, become appliances, metaphorical human iPods that can furnish neutral background music or generate playlists with the latest and greatest styles that will increase attendance and membership.

But as the title of this book indicates, the work of church musicians is more about content than style, more about vocation than occupation, more about the relationship with one's community than about the music itself. It is about the people of God—the angels, the saints, the "myriads of myriads and thousands of thousands," and "every creature in heaven and on earth and under the earth and in the sea" (Rev. 5:11, 13)—who sing. Their song—God's song, our song—is an earthly foretaste of the heavenly feast where all are lost in wonder, love, and praise. As the poster on the next page from the Association of Lutheran Church Musicians reminds us, the church musician's vocation is a worthy service to God, God's people, and the world. It is, indeed, a high and holy calling.

When Christ's people, the baptized,
gather for worship
they receive God's love
in word and sacrament,
and through the gift of music,
pray, praise, proclaim & recount
the story of God's grace in song.

The cantor...
the historical term
among Lutherans,
is the leader
of the people's song.

THE ROLE OF THE CANTOR

The cantor
is responsible
for leading
the
musical
expression
of the people...the
assembly, choral
groups, solo singers, &
instrumentalists, among
whom organists have
been especially
important for Lutherans.

The cantor uses whatever musical
resources are available,
using them in a manner appropriate
to the talents of those serving and the
needs of the people who are served.

The cantor's work
is a worthy
service to God,
God's people,
and
the world.

The cantor leads
the earthly assembly
in a foretaste of
John's vision of the heavenly assembly
in which all creatures give
praise, honor, glory and power
to the Lamb.

—IT IS A HIGH AND HOLY CALLING—

Adapted from "The Role of the Cantor" poster, designed by Ann Siverling Kirchhoff, courtesy of the Association of Lutheran Church Musicians.

The church musician's vocation is contextual

As indicated by the scenarios that began this prelude, the church musician's vocation is shaped by local context—the people served, their piety, their heritage, their languages and dialects, the spaces in which they gather, the surrounding neighborhood, and so much more. Moreover, contexts are always changing. The local, national, and international circumstances that surround the singing of God's people are always in flux. Some cause us to cry out with psalms of lament, some with hymns of thanksgiving, and others with songs that proclaim God's justice. And within each assembly are layers of constant change: baptisms, life passages, academic milestones, times of planting and harvest, transitions in leadership, and more than we can yet imagine or name. Alongside the ebbs and flows of changing contexts, the focus of assembly song moves with the cycles and seasons of the church year.

The array of possibilities in each and every context together pose a welcome challenge to labels that compartmentalize the singing of God's people into simplistic and insufficient categories such as traditional, contemporary, low- and high-church, liturgical and nonliturgical, and so forth. These labels can easily become distractions and obstructions, tempting us to focus more on styles and material trappings than on the means of grace. We would do well to let go of them and, in their place, embrace all that proclaims Christ in word and sacrament. Like faith, contextual discernment is not easy; attitudes such as "we've always done it this way" or "let's throw out the playbook and change everything" are, in most cases, excuses that prevent us from appreciating contextual richness. Like the church, context is both messy and beautiful, treasured and troubled, and resists our feeble attempts to preserve or institutionalize it. Our contexts revolve around Christ who was, is, and is to come. How can this give us faith to sing at all times and in all places even as contexts change?

The church musician (cantor) attends to the voice of the gathered assembly

Like the poster shown on page 14, this book frequently refers to church musicians as cantors, the historical term for musicians in the Lutheran church. The word *cantor* is derived from the Latin verb *cantāre* (meaning "to sing") and serves as a reminder of the church musician's most important task—to lead assembly song. Descriptions of Christian cantors can be found in documents from the fourth, fifth, and sixth centuries. Even before that, Israelite musicians who led the singing of psalms were known as *hazzān*, a plural form of *cantor* in Hebrew. During the Reformation, Martin Luther expressed a need for cantors who could teach singing in their communities, as well as compose hymns to be sung in worship and at home. Today cantors serve as organists, pianists, guitarists, singers, percussionists, conductors, and more. Regardless of their gifts, training, or abilities, all use their time and talents to equip, support, and nurture the voice of the singing assembly. All are cantors. The hymns and songs mentioned on the pages that follow do not presume one specific type or style of accompaniment, and use of the term *cantor* for leading assembly song is meant to invite a range of creative, contextual possibilities.

The church musician's craft is rooted in the liturgy and the lectionary

The ideas in this book presume use of the Revised Common Lectionary, an ecumenical, three-year cycle of readings upon which *Evangelical Lutheran Worship*, *Sundays and Seasons*, and their attendant resources are based. This common set of readings serves the unity of the church and is a sturdy center from which proclamation, prayer, and preaching emanate. In *A Three-Year Banquet: The Lectionary for the Assembly*, Gail Ramshaw reminds us that the lectionary is not just for preachers and musicians, nor is it merely a specialized catalog of sermon and song ideas. Rather, she writes, "Use of a lectionary makes clear to the entire baptized assembly that the Bible is the book of all the people."[3] And, as explained in *Principles for Worship*, the lectionary serves "as a source of language and imagery for worship texts and hymnody, as a foundation for formation and devotional reflection, and as a sign of unity."[4]

3 Gail Ramshaw, *A Three-Year Banquet: The Lectionary for the Assembly* (Minneapolis: Augsburg Fortress, 2004), 13.

4 Evangelical Lutheran Church in America, *Renewing Worship, Vol. 2: Principles for Worship* (Minneapolis: Augsburg Fortress, 2002), 8.

Similar principles apply to patterns for worship and liturgical wisdom that the church has accumulated across the centuries. "The church has gravitated to liturgical forms," writes Paul Westermeyer, in order to "check our egos, to keep us from assaulting ourselves and one another with our personalities and personal agendas, and to point insofar as we are able to God in Christ from whom through the Spirit all blessings flow."[5] Or, as ELCA Presiding Bishop Elizabeth Eaton wrote in 2015, "There is a certain humility and beautiful communion in not trying to reinvent the service each time, but to join with brothers and sisters throughout the world and across the centuries."[6] While special Sunday emphases such as Youth Sunday, Pledge Sunday, Rally Sunday, Music Sunday, or World Communion Sunday may be well intended, the lectionary calls us to remember that care for youth and the marginalized, the stewardship of all creation, and praise of God through music and the arts are *ongoing* concerns in the life of the church. Like a ground bass in music, the lectionary and liturgy anchor and support us even though our surroundings change from measure to measure, from Sunday to Sunday, from year to year.

---

5   Paul Westermeyer, *Rise, O Church: Reflections on the Church, Its Music, and Empire* (St. Louis: MorningStar Music Publishers, 2008), 7.

6   Elizabeth Eaton, "Worship Is the Heart of All We Do," *The Lutheran* (May 2015), 50.

The cantor is called to love God's people

To be a church musician is to enter into a relationship—personal, pastoral, theological—with one's community, not just its music. A wise colleague and friend once quoted a mentor who said: "To be a church musician, you must love the people *more* than you love the music."

Ideas gleaned from a book cannot substitute for the experience of knowing a community, and a book as short as this can only begin to scratch the surface. Perhaps you will find it too vague, and frustratingly so; should that happen, consult the resources listed in the footnotes and at the end of each chapter. Yet even if this were a multivolume resource brimming with footnotes and musical examples, it would still remain inadequate because it does not know you nor the community you serve. Use this book as a means of thinking about the relational, communal, and formative power of music, not just choices (important as they are) about hymns, liturgy settings, anthems, preludes, and postludes.

> Use the ideas and questions posed here to develop new and better ideas and questions about your community's voice and its song. Equip and nurture their voices. Bless their singing.

The cantor and assembly song:
principles

It is not I who sing, but the church.[1]
—Dietrich Bonhoeffer

The cantor's principal task is not to offer flawless postludes and stirring anthems, or to administer a bustling music program but, rather, to care for the singing (cantāre) of the assembly that gathers for worship. Instruments and choirs may assist in leading assembly song, but as *Principles for Worship* instructs, "the assembly is the primary musical ensemble, and its song is the core of all music in worship."[2] Like conductors who prepare to lead ensembles, before cantors can select music or

---

1   Dietrich Bonhoeffer, *Life Together; Prayerbook of the Bible* (Minneapolis: Fortress Press, 1996), 68.

2   *Renewing Worship 2: Principles for Worship* (Minneapolis: Augsburg Fortress, 2002), Principle M-3.

begin rehearsal they must know something—hopefully many things—about the assemblies they serve.

Attending to the assembly

The assembly—again, the primary musical ensemble—includes children of God of all ages, siblings in Christ. When they gather, they assemble a vast array of experiences, stories, abilities, and feelings. Among the assembly may be longtime members who were baptized, confirmed, or married in the building where you serve; the widow whose spouse is inurned in the church's columbarium; first-time visitors; refugees; political activists; a couple contemplating divorce; those with anxieties about their employment; a same-sex couple preparing to adopt a child; the hard-of-hearing choir member; those with food insecurity; those overstimulated by technology; or those questioning their faith.

As cantor you must love every one of them and work to develop an awareness of the perspectives they bring to communal singing. For example, briefly consider:

- Do the words of psalms, hymns, and anthems in your setting acknowledge or honor the experiences of all God's people, or only a select few?
- Do the authors, translators, and composers in your assembly's core repertoire reflect the diversity of God's creation, or only a small segment?
- Is it appropriate to presume that everyone can read notation, that everyone can see a screen from a distance, or

that everyone has the strength to hold a hymnal or other worship book?

- With whom in your assembly can you discuss these or similar questions?

You may have noticed that those questions aren't really about the music itself. Before cantors can think about musical choices and leadership, they must know their people, contexts, and physical spaces. As with rehearsing and performing a musical work, cantors must always be listening too! The breadth and depth required by attentive listening may require cantors to sometimes approach their craft as if they were anthropologists or ethnomusicologists, experiencing and observing a community's values, habits, practices, behaviors, and adaptation to the worship space—all of which can inform musical decisions. For example:

- Does the community tend to gather in reverent silence or exchange boisterous greetings? What does this mean for the appropriateness of an instrumental prelude or a call-and-response gathering song?
- How does a cantor honor, expand, or even challenge a community's pride in its traditional ethnic heritage, language, values, or other local customs?
- How might a community's communion practices affect musical choices? Does it really make sense to introduce a new hymn when most of the assembly is already at the table, being ushered toward the table, or praying silently?
- Can the choir assist in strengthening spoken texts and

acclamations in a challenging acoustic? Responses such as "Thanks be to God" and "Amen, come, Lord Jesus" also have musical rhythms, contours, and accents!

- On a day when assembly singing felt cautious or hesitant, was that because of the hymns themselves—perhaps a new, unfamiliar tune—or because of inadequate introductions, unclear timing between stanzas, or bland organ registration? Was it the weather? Did low barometric pressure during a heavy rain make everyone seem drowsy and sluggish? Or was it a combination of everything?

As will be discussed in chapter 4, to fully attend to the assembly—to be able to ask these and related questions—cantors, pastors, and other church leaders need to be willing and able to shrug off their own pride and personal preferences and, instead, work to empower the assembly. They must possess the humility to give themselves over to the experience of others, to step out of their own comfort zones. In *The Pastor: A Spirituality*, Gordon Lathrop offers advice to pastors that is equally applicable to cantors: "A responsible [cantor] will be learning how to value his own wisdom, while also knowing what a fool he is, how to value her own kindness, while also knowing that she cannot be the All-friend."[3] Once, when asked how he prepared sermons, Lathrop responded with advice that is equally applicable to the preparation of music by cantors: "I try to pay attention," he wrote, and "attend to the texts that are going to be read, to the people who are going to gather and to the purpose of

---

3   Gordon W. Lathrop, *The Pastor: A Spirituality* (Minneapolis: Fortress Press, 2006), 13.

their gathering, and to the world in which they gather."[4] This ethnographic, assembly-centered approach is also emphasized in the *Musicians Guide to Evangelical Lutheran Worship*: "Know the worshiping community you serve," advise the authors. Moreover, "familiarize yourself with their existing repertoire, their cultural heritage, their likes and dislikes."[5] In other words, attend to the people of God in your assembly before you decide what to sing and how to lead that song.

Selecting assembly song

Choices about assembly song emerge from complex, interlocking webs of relationships that revolve around the lectionary and the news, and any unique occurrences (e.g., service of healing; affirmation of baptism; a recent tragedy in the community), as well as the community's ability, memory, spaces, instruments, and other matters of context.

Think for a moment of a tree as representative of assembly song: The trunk represents the entire corpus of available hymns and songs. It's an enormous tree, a giant sequoia! Its branches reach out in many different directions like section headings of a hymnal—large branches for Advent, Holy Baptism, Healing, Stewardship, Creation, and Prayer. Perhaps smaller branches are individual hymns: a branch for "Earth and all stars!" (ELW 731) and a branch for "God of the sparrow" (ELW 740) that

4   *The Pastor: A Spirituality*, 55.

5   Jennifer Baker-Trinity, Scott C. Weidler, and Robert Buckley Farlee, eds., *Musicians Guide to Evangelical Lutheran Worship* (Minneapolis: Augsburg Fortress, 2007), 3.

are connected to the larger Creation branch. Some of these smaller, hymn-sized branches provide nourishing and sustaining fruit—a phrase, image, or idea that continues to provide food for thought long after the hymn has ended: God as jeweler (ELW 736), Christ as holy Vine and living Tree (ELW 447), or a mothering Spirit (ELW 397).

And beneath the visible portions of the tree is a root system that spreads far and wide, feeding and supporting the trunk with tangled networks composed of musical styles, the lectionary and church year, and the life of the local community. Through passing years and succeeding generations, the root systems and branches grow. Some fare better than others. Some produce more fruit and offer more shade and shelter. Some wither and fade. The ecosystem changes slowly. Such is the situation with assembly song. Cantors must be mindful of the whole tree—what it offers, its cycles of growth, and how best to tend it.

And for the hymns and songs used in a single service, consider the analogy of a well-balanced meal. There are lighter and heavier courses—entrées, vegetable dishes, and desserts. Some courses use treasured family recipes while others offer something new and adventurous. The host attends to allergies and sensitivities, too, but in a way that still allows every guest to be at the same table and share the meal together.

Assembly song too can function like a well-balanced meal. There are meaty entrées such as Reformation-era chorales with longer tunes and rich content spread across several stanzas; just as a good entrée may take a while to eat, these chorales take a while to sing! There are hymns and songs with fewer stanzas, their shorter phrases perhaps spiced with a refrain that can be sung in a language other than English: "¡Aleluya! Cristo resucitó" (ELW 375); "Njoo kwetu, Roho mwema" (ELW 401); "Gaudeamus Domino" (ELW 506). There are hymns that challenge our complacency and comfort—tough to swallow, but healthy for our diet. There's lighter fare, too, such as choruses or ostinatos whose repetition invites focus on a sole image or single verse of scripture. Like a purée or garnish—or whipped cream on a dessert—they can enhance flavor and offer contrast. However, one cannot subsist on a diet of whipped cream alone.

With these images and metaphors in mind—or perhaps other comparisons that are more appropriate for your context—let us turn to some specifics about what to sing.

Hymn of the Day

Considerations about assembly song often begin with the hymn of the day, a practice that began early in the Reformation. For early Lutherans, this hymn (then called *de tempore*, or "of the time") sought to unpack the day's readings and preaching emphases most directly. Today some may know this as a "sermon hymn" because of its proximity and close relationship to the sermon. Accordingly, attentive worship planners are encouraged to view the sermon and hymn of the day together as a single unit.

The hymn of the day should be planned as far in advance as is possible or practical. (The practice of sending a list of Sunday's hymns to the musician just a few days before the service is highly discouraged!) For musicians, advance planning facilitates selection and preparation of related preludes, stanza settings, instrumental descants, and other service music. Once the hymn of the day is determined, other hymns and songs can be selected, at the same time or later in the planning process. Also consider the importance of balance. Perhaps a shorter hymn of the day allows for a longer gathering hymn. Maybe a longer hymn of the day can be balanced by shorter hymns and songs—perhaps a Taizé chant—elsewhere in the service. Perhaps a hymn of the day that introduces an unfamiliar text or tune encourages more familiar choices for other songs the assembly will sing in that service.

However, even the most thoughtful plans can be upended by a significant event in the community or in the wider world. In these instances, cantors should respect ways in which pastors want to adapt or rewrite their sermons. Likewise, pastors should respect the planning that musicians have invested in a particular hymn of the day and its balance with other parts of the service. Whether planned weeks or days in advance, choices about the hymn of the day should always grow out of honest and healthy conversation.

Other hymns and songs

Other hymns and songs radiate outward from the gravitas of the sermon and hymn of the day pairing, perhaps emphasizing or unpacking images and metaphors from the readings, events and occasions in the community's life, or other seasonal emphases.

As previously suggested, it is helpful to think about different types of balance within a given day's menu of hymn and song selections. Singing several multi-stanza hymns from the nineteenth century runs the risk of becoming wearisome and tedious. Conversely, a service of shorter, repetitive songs may ultimately feel anticlimactic or unfulfilling. Although shorter songs work well as prayer responses and acclamations, their compact texts do not always fully engage with the richness of the lectionary readings and preaching emphases when they are used at the gathering, offertory, sending, and as the hymn of the day.

Musicians should also plan to avoid vocal fatigue in the assembly: multiple stanzas of a long tune with a high range can tire even the most able singers. For longer hymns, consider offering momentary points of rest by assigning different stanzas to different groups (using inclusive designations such as "high voices" or "treble voices" and "low voices" instead of "women" and "men"), or by using a choral, instrumental, or keyboard setting, either composed or improvised. For example:

"Thy strong word" (ELW 511)
Stanza 1	All
Stanza 2	Lower Voices; All at "Alleluia"
Stanza 3	Choir
Stanza 4	Treble Voices; All at "Alleluia"
Stanzas 5, 6	All

"O God, our help in ages past" (ELW 632)
Stanza 1	All, in unison
Stanzas 2–4	All, in harmony
Stanza 5	Organ
Stanza 6	All, in unison

"Oh, praise the gracious power" (ELW 651)
Stanzas 1, 2	All
Stanza 3	Organ
Stanza 4	Treble Voices
Stanza 5	Lower Voices
Stanzas 6, 7	All

Cantors will also want to consider the benefits and challenges associated with singing in unison and harmony. The *Musicians Guide to Evangelical Lutheran Worship* presents some considerations:

- What is the character of the tune? Long, floating lines? Rhythmically energetic phrases?
- Does harmony potentially slow down or add weight to a lighter melody?

- Is it better sung in unison or is harmony a necessary element? Does it come from a genre that prefers one or the other?
- Might the group prefer to sing in harmony? Are they able to do it well?
- Might singing in harmony intimidate some and hinder the song?
- What kind of accompaniments might be possible if the group sings in harmony?
- Might an accompaniment be different if they are singing in unison?
- Could I do something in my accompaniment that might help the group's endeavor to sing in harmony?
- Might the assembly even be able to "go it alone," [and] sing without any instrumental leadership?[6]

If your context allows for many different styles of musical leadership, consider emphasizing this abundance of musical expression by including songs such as a sixteenth-century chorale, a Taizé chant, a piano-led ballad, and a paperless song all in the same service. Like the depth and breadth of prayer intercessions, such musical combinations can hold a day's lectionary and preaching themes together alongside concerns for the church, creation, nations, and congregation without reverting to tokenism or to separate services for different styles. Cantors should also attend to the overall balance of authors, translators, composers, geographical sources, and time periods in song choices for single services as well as

6   *Musicians Guide to Evangelical Lutheran Worship*, 28.

throughout seasons of the liturgical year. The church has been blessed with a treasury of songs by writers and composers of color, women, and members of marginalized communities. What does it suggest to the assembly when its songs only represent Caucasian males of European descent? This diversity—stylistic, geographical, temporal, linguistic—sung by one assembly in its time and place, points toward the unity in Christ shared across the wider church and celebrates the manifold gifts of the Spirit.

Across several years of crafting texts for assembly song, hymn writer Susan Palo Cherwien has developed a "sieve of seven questions" that pastors and cantors will find useful for selecting hymns, as well as for virtually any decision that shapes the assembly's singing and its worship. "They are good questions to ask," she writes, "regarding visual art, the way print looks on a page, for vestments and flowers and worship space. Good questions for music." And, she adds, "they are pretty good questions for most of life, too."[7] The questions are:

> Is it true?
> Is it beautiful?
> Is it excellent?
> Does it give God glory?
> Can it bear the weight of mystery?
> Is it appropriate?
> Does it replace something of greater worth?

7   Susan Palo Cherwien, "The Sieve of Seven Questions," *CrossAccent: Journal of the Association of Lutheran Church Musicians* 27.2 (Summer 2019), 40.

Worship leaders do well to remember that they are probably more familiar with their setting's primary worship resource(s) than many in the assembly. What may seem trite or too familiar for the pastor or cantor may, in fact, be a welcome entry point or fresh image for longtime members and first-time visitors.

Cantors would also do well to compile and maintain a list of "core" hymns and songs that are familiar to their communities. Perhaps such a list can be created together with pastors, choir members, other worship leaders, or even the entire assembly. Records of hymns and songs used in worship can be marked in a hymnal set aside for this purpose, or entered into a spreadsheet or other list; this practice is particularly useful for helping new cantors better understand the assemblies they have been called to serve. The process of hymn selection for each service may begin with this list, and may gently guide planners away from selecting too many new songs all at once. Such a list may also show areas where an assembly has room to grow, perhaps by learning stanzas or a refrain in a new language or by singing hymns that utilize expanded language and images for God.[8] New hymns can be introduced in many ways, and repetition is key: a new song might be heard one week as a choir anthem, its melody featured the next week as part of the prelude, its text quoted another week in a sermon, its meaning explored yet another week in a worship folder note, social media post, or news-

---

8   See Brian Wentzel, "Curating the Core Hymns of Your Congregation," *CrossAccent: Journal of the Association of Lutheran Church Musicians* 27.3 (Fall–Winter 2019), 40–47.

letter reflection—all before text and tune are voiced by the assembly. Introduced carefully and gradually, new hymns can begin to feel like those old, familiar favorites.

Assembly song at weddings and funerals

Cantors are also called to lead songs that sing of God's love, faithfulness, and promise of resurrection at occasional services of the church such as weddings and funerals. Although selecting and leading assembly song for these services reflects considerations made for the Sunday assembly, the likely presence of visitors unaccustomed to communal singing and involvement of other planners—family members, wedding coordinators, and funeral directors—may require thoughtful conversation about the importance of assembly song, perhaps even foundational conversations about the nature of worship itself.

Weddings and funerals sometimes require pastors, musicians, and other church leaders to serve as advocates for the assembly and for one another, especially if they are viewed as trappings alongside apparel, flowers, and other pre-purchased commodities that obscure and dishonor the Christian witness due the moment. Musicians, in particular, are often asked to play innocuous background music or accompany theologically vapid pop songs wherein sentiment, nostalgia, and other nebulous aesthetic feelings are prioritized over content; the loving promises of God, the death and resurrection of Jesus, and the comfort of the Spirit are, in essence, negligible, as is the presence and participation of the assembly. However, worship leaders are called to sing a different and often countercultural tune, a counter-melody to cultural demands. In concert with pastors and other planners, cantors can help show how these services proclaim God's love in Christ in the midst of the gathered assembly. Or, as introductions to the marriage and funeral liturgies in *Evangelical Lutheran Worship* make plain:

> The church in worship surrounds these [marriage] promises with the gathering of God's people, the witness of the word of God, and prayers of blessing and intercession. (*ELW*, p. 286)

> When the church gathers to mark the end of life, Christ crucified and risen is the witness of worship, the strength of mutual consolation, and the hope of healing. (*ELW*, p. 279)

The ability of pastors and cantors to plan assembly-oriented liturgies for marriages and funerals is not only dependent on thoughtful conversations with families and service industry professionals, but is also shaped by ways congregations administer their facilities. In some settings rental fees are assessed for use of the building. While a congregation may depend on this income for financial stability, this practice can sometimes reinforce the notion that pastors and musicians are vendors who, in turn, are expected to acquiesce to demands of their paying customers. Conversely, some settings understand weddings and funerals as ministries of the congregation and wider church, and no fees are charged for the use of facilities or for the participation of the pastor, cantor, altar guild, and sexton.

Regardless of approach, it is beneficial for pastors, musicians, and other worship leaders to work together to craft written guidance for these services that, whether used privately among staff or posted publicly on the church's website, honors both God and the worship of the gathered assembly. Both the marriage and funeral planning handbooks listed in this chapter's resources contain helpful advice, supplemental materials, and music suggestions for such a process. In particular, musicians may wish to consider the appropriateness of the following:

- Beginning their planning conversations with choices about assembly song rather than processionals and recessionals
- Replacing instrumental preludes, processionals, or recessionals with assembly song
- Attending to other spoken and sung acclamations and affirmations voiced by the assembly
- Modeling language that focuses on worship and the assembly rather than ceremonial elements
- Developing relationships and maintaining dialogue with local funeral directors or wedding coordinators in order to understand each other's assumptions about local traditions, best practices, remuneration, and the like

No matter the context or circumstance, musicians should—and perhaps most importantly—be prepared to teach throughout the planning process, to always point to the crucified and risen

Christ as the witness of worship. In the *Evangelical Lutheran Worship* funeral liturgy, the thanksgiving for baptism acclaims that God's breath gave us life. That living and saving breath of the triune God is the story we sing along our baptismal journeys—at gatherings, sendings, baptisms, weddings, funerals, and each week around word and sacrament where we join the unending hymn of the angelic choir and the church: "Holy, holy, holy Lord, God of power and might, heaven and earth are full of your glory!" Of our story and song in this time and place, Susan Palo Cherwien reminds us:

We who sing these words together
are people of story
When we sing together
we are bards
the story singers
the wisdom keepers
chanting the story
as around the sparkling fire
singing the story
that has made us a people
singing the wisdom
so that the next seven generations
can find their way
and not be lost
so that the generations yet to come
not forget the ancestral foraging grounds
not forget where to shelter from storm
not forget the way to water.
We who sing this story
God's story—
together
God's story in Christ
together—
we are transformed into a community
of memory
of future
of a transformed
and holy
now.[9]

9 Susan Palo Cherwien, *From Glory into Glory: Reflections for Worship* (St. Louis: MorningStar
   Music Publishers, 2009), 286. Used by permission.

Resources

Books

- Brueggemann, Walter. *A Glad Obedience: Why and What We Sing*. Louisville, KY: Westminster John Knox Press, 2019.
- Consultation on Common Texts. *The Revised Common Lectionary: Twentieth Anniversary Annotated Edition*. Minneapolis: Augsburg Fortress, 2012.
- Gray, Scotty. *Hermeneutics of Hymnody: A Comprehensive and Integrated Approach to Understanding Hymns*. Macon, GA: Smyth and Helwys, 2015.
- Kubicki, Judith M. *The Song of the Singing Assembly: A Theology of Christian Hymnody*. Chicago: GIA Publications, 2017.
- Quivik, Melinda A. *Remembering God's Promises: A Funeral Planning Handbook*. Minneapolis: Augsburg Fortress, 2018.
- Rimbo, Robert A. *Why Worship Matters*. Minneapolis: Augsburg Fortress, 2004.
- Walters, Paul E. *Love and Faithfulness: A Marriage Planning Handbook*. Minneapolis: Augsburg Fortress, 2018.

Websites

- Association of Lutheran Church Musicians, "Statement on Worship and Music," https://alcm.org/about/worship_statement/.
- Evangelical Lutheran Church in America, "Frequently Asked Questions" (Worship), https://www.elca.org/worshipfaq.

Assembly song collections

- *Hear Our Prayer: Sung Responses for Chorus and Assembly.* Minneapolis: Augsburg Fortress, 2007.
- *Music Sourcebook for Life Passages: Healing, Funeral, and Marriage.* Minneapolis: Augsburg Fortress, 2018.
- *Singing in Community: Paperless Music for Worship.* Minneapolis: Augsburg Fortress, 2017

The cantor and assembly song:
applications

The preceding chapter offered suggestions for ways pastors, cantors, and worship leaders can approach the task of selecting assembly song. But how does this actually work in practice? After discussing one specific lectionary example, this chapter takes a closer look at the musical richness of two additional opportunities for assembly singing: the chanting of psalms, and music during communion.

Hymns and songs for the Baptism of Our Lord

Let's return to the beginning of this book and the cantors who were preparing to lead assembly song for the Baptism of Our Lord. What considerations might guide choices for assembly singing on this day across all three cycles of the Revised Common Lectionary?

The day and its readings

Just as a preacher's sermon begins with the study of text, so, too, does the selection of assembly song. Consider these key questions or others like them:

- What are the texts for the day?
- What are some notable keywords, verbs, actions, rituals, or other images in these stories?
- How do these readings connect with our own lives, communities, and ministries?
- What insights are offered by commentaries such as *Sundays and Seasons: Preaching?*

A scan of the Propers section in the front of *Evangelical Lutheran Worship* (p. 22) indicates that the texts for the Baptism of Our Lord are:

Year A	Year B	Year C
Isaiah 42:1-9	Genesis 1:1-5	Isaiah 43:1-7
Psalm 29	Psalm 29	Psalm 29
Acts 10:34-43	Acts 19:1-7	Acts 8:14-17
Matthew 3:13-17	Mark 1:4-11	Luke 3:15-17, 21-22

To begin, what can we observe in the texts themselves?

Justice is a prominent theme in the readings for year A. Isaiah tells how God's servant will "bring forth justice to the nations" (Isa. 42:1, 3), and in the second reading this is precisely what Peter tells the Roman centurion and his household of the congregation that proclaim God's justice in the world.

In the readings for year B, the Spirit is a central character. The Spirit is present in the wind sweeping over the primordial waters (Gen. 1:2), at baptisms Paul performed in Ephesus (Acts 19:6), and at Jesus' own baptism by John in the Jordan (Mark 1:10). Perhaps on this day choices about assembly song can be guided by consideration of how we sing about the presence and work of the Spirit—not just at baptism but also in our vocations, in times of discernment, in worship, and throughout our lives, both as individuals and as communities.

The power and splendor of God's voice (Ps. 29) is woven throughout the readings for year C. God's voice calls us by name (Isa. 43:1) and calls all people—from north, south, east, west, and all the ends of the earth (Isa. 43:5-6). With vivid verbs the psalmist recounts the strength and glory of the Lord's voice: it thunders, breaks, shakes, bursts forth in lightning flashes, and strips the forest bare. Like the gospel readings from Matthew and Mark in years A and B, Luke recounts the voice of God declaring at Jesus' baptism: "You are my Son, the Beloved; with you I am well pleased" (Luke 3:22). The triune God knows us by name and promises to be with us always.

Images in the readings

After reading and contemplating the lectionary readings, begin thinking about sections of *Evangelical Lutheran Worship* that best relate to the day's themes and actions. For example:

- What sections of the hymnal contain stanzas that resonate with these readings, themes, and images?

- What keywords from the topical index (*ELW*, pp. 1178–1188) yield compelling choices for this day and its readings?
- Are there hymns and songs that also bring the day's ritual actions into perspective?

In year A, a scan of the Holy Baptism (ELW 442–459) and Commitment, Discipleship (ELW 796–818) sections may yield suggestions such as the following:

- "We are baptized in Christ Jesus" (ELW 451) for the mention of water, witness, and new beginnings, as well as the breaking of bread
- "Rise, shine, you people!" (ELW 665) not only for its "light" imagery appropriate for the Time after Epiphany, but also for its progression toward new creation in stanza 4
- "We raise our hands to you, O Lord" (ELW 690), for combined imagery about springs, new creation, and ministry
- "Let justice flow like streams" (ELW 717)
- "In Christ called to baptize" (ELW 575), which sings of both holy baptism and holy communion
- The refrain in "Lord, you give the great commission" (ELW 579), which reminds us of our baptismal calling: "With the Spirit's gifts empower us for the work of ministry"

In year B, the Holy Baptism (ELW 442–459) and Pentecost, Holy Spirit (ELW 395–407) sections might provide fruitful options such as these:

- "Crashing waters at creation" (ELW 455) for a connection to the Genesis reading

- The image of the descending dove in stanza 3 of "Praise and thanksgiving be to God" (ELW 458)
- "This is the Spirit's entry now" (ELW 448)
- The mention of baptismal waters in "O living breath of God" (ELW 407)
- "When Jesus came to Jordan" (ELW 305), which also invokes the Day of Pentecost in stanza 3, a connection that is surely worth singing about

And in year C one could consider options from the Holy Trinity (ELW 408–415) and Creation (ELW 730–740) sections. For example:

- The rousing text of "I bind unto myself today" (ELW 450) is a wonderful confluence of the day's themes; its Irish melody sings at both stately and brisk tempos, perhaps accompanied by organ, by guitar and fiddle, or even by both in alternation.
- Three stanzas of "Go, my children, with my blessing" (ELW 543) recall the splendor and power of God's voice sung in the day's psalm, and stanza 1 offers a fitting connection (and conclusion) to the day's liturgy: "In my love's baptismal river I have made you mine forever."
- The song "Many will come," in *Music Sourcebook: All Saints through Transfiguration*, repeats all of the cardinal directions heard in the Isaiah reading: "Many will come from east and west, and from north and south, to be washed in the waters of life."

The sturdy and vigorous melody of "Many will come" is fitting for a procession to or from the font, perhaps at the Thanksgiving for Baptism (*ELW*, p. 97) during the beginning of the liturgy or at the Affirmation of Baptism (*ELW*, p. 234) after the hymn of the day is sung. In addition to these options, perhaps you, your pastor, staff colleagues, or choir members can think of many others—hymns and songs you have sung time and time again whose language, imagery, and text-tune pairings have taken hold in the assembly's imagination and heart.

Additional hymns and songs

After developing a list of preliminary options, it may be help-ful to consult other resources such as *Indexes to Evangelical Lutheran Worship, Choosing Contemporary Music: Seasonal, Topical, Lectionary Indexes*, and *Sundays and Seasons: Guide to Worship Planning*. From a scan of these resources, the preceding lists could be expanded to include additional styles and images in hymns and songs, such as:

Year A
"Christ, when for us you were baptized" (ELW 304)
"Come to the water" (MSB2 S562)
"Jesus, the light of the world" (TFF 59)
"Songs of thankfulness and praise" (ELW 310)
"The only Son from heaven" (ELW 309)
"When Jesus came to Jordan" (ELW 305)

Year B
"Baptized and Set Free" (ELW 453)
"Go, my children, with my blessing" (ELW 543)
"I'm going on a journey" (ELW 446)
"I've just come from the fountain" (TFF 111)
"Light shone in darkness" (ELW 307)

Year C
"All who believe and are baptized" (ELW 442)
"Here, O Lord, your servants gather" (ELW 530)
"Spirit of God, descend upon my heart" (ELW 800)
"You Are Mine" (ELW 581)

Singing breadth and depth

Once a working list of options has been assembled, it's time for the preacher, cantor, and additional planners to discuss suitable options for the hymn of the day. As discussed in the previous chapter, this is one of the most important musical decisions for any service, a focal point that guides subsequent planning. After selecting a hymn of the day, consider other hymns, songs, and styles that might provide reinforcement, contrast, and an appropriate balance (depending, of course, on context) between local and global expressions, the musical gifts and abilities of the assembly and its song leaders, the community's "core" repertoire of hymns and songs, and the attributes of the space where the assembly gathers for worship. For example, one of many configurations could be the following:

Year A	Year B	Year C
Gathering "I bind unto myself today" (ELW 450)	**Gathering** "Crashing waters at creation" (ELW 455)	**Thanksgiving for Baptism** (Consider singing "Many will come" as a procession to the font)
Hymn of the Day "In Christ called to baptize" (ELW 575)	**Hymn of the Day** "I'm going on a journey" (ELW 446) Consider printing this hymn in the worship folder so the assembly can sing while gathering around the font for the Affirmation of Baptism	**Gathering** "All who believe and are baptized" (ELW 442) Consider an extended introduction that allows the assembly enough time to return to their seats in order to open their hymnals for the singing of the hymn.
Communion "We are baptized in Christ Jesus" (ELW 451)		
Sending "Let justice flow like streams" (ELW 717)	**Communion** "Baptized and Set Free" (ELW 453)	**Hymn of the Day** "O blessed spring" (ELW 447)
	Sending "I've just come from the fountain" (TFF 111)	**Communion** "I come with joy" (ELW 482)
		Sending "Go, my children, with my blessing" (ELW 543)

Your list will, of course, differ from the list crafted by those working down the street or in the next town. The core repertoires of the assemblies served by the four musicians described in the prelude (see p. 9) require distinct approaches for the same set of lectionary readings. The best lectionary match is not always the most familiar, nor is it always the most appropriate choice for the instruments available and the acoustics of a given location. And, as mentioned in the previous chapter, significant local, national, or international events—natural disasters, violence, civil unrest—may suddenly cast the lectionary in a new light and require leaders to carefully reconsider existing plans. While planning and preparation are essential for leading assembly song, so also is the capacity to be nimble and accommodating with one's plans.

The abundance of images and ideas for each set of lectionary readings is reflected in the title of a hymn—"So much to sing about"—written by Jaroslav Vajda (1919–2008) to mark the seventieth birthday of Paul Manz:

> So much to sing about,
> So much to praise you for,
> So much I cannot live without
> And so much more:
> At which display
> Of majesty
> The very stones are moved to shout.

So much to sing about:
All I have seen and heard,
Your glory in my talents' use
My best reward:
That others see
What I have seen
And sing with me: "It is the Lord!"[1]

Indeed, there is much to sing *about*, and so much to *sing* too! As Vajda's text poignantly reminds us, planners who choose and lead the Spirit-filled songs of their assemblies do not seek to glorify themselves, their favorites, or their instruments. Instead, they invite voices of all ages and abilities to join that magnificent hymn of all creation which, in all times and places, proclaims: "Blessing, honor, glory, and might be to God and the Lamb forever. Amen."

Psalmody

The church with psalms must shout:
no door can keep them out.[2]
—George Herbert

The psalms are not only an important part of the church's lectionary; they speak vividly to our full gamut of emotions. Martin

1   Jaroslav J. Vajda, "So Much to Sing About." Text © 1989 Concordia Publishing House. Used with permission.

2   George Herbert, 1593–1633, "Let All the World in Every Corner Sing," in *The Temple* (Cambridge, 1633), 45.

Luther called the collection "a fine enchiridion or handbook," adding that "anyone who could not read the whole Bible would here have anyway almost an entire summary of it, comprised in one little book."[3] John Calvin remarked that reading the psalter was akin to "re-reading his own life story,"[4] and Paul Westermeyer rightly observes that the psalms "are in the blood of the church," and, as such, "are the source of its hymnody."[5] Long before these writers, Ambrose, a fourth-century bishop of Milan, wrote:

> A psalm is the blessing of the people, the praise of God, the commendation of the multitude, the applause of all, the speech of every person, the voice of the church, the sonorous profession of faith, devotion full of authority, the joy of liberty, the noise of good cheer, and the echo of gladness. It softens anger, it gives release from anxiety, it alleviates sorrow; it is protection at night, instruction by day, a shield in time of fear, a feast of holiness, the image of tranquility, a pledge of peace and harmony, which produces one song from various and sundry voices in the manner of a cithara. The day's dawning resounds with a psalm, with a psalm its passing echoes.[6]

3 Martin Luther, "Preface to the Psalter," in *Luther's Works, Vol. 35, Word and Sacrament I*, ed. Theodore Bachman (Philadelphia: Fortress Press, 1960), 254–257.

4 John Calvin, quoted in C. Hassell Bullock, "The Psalms and Faith/Tradition," in *The Psalms: Language for All Seasons of the Soul*, ed. Andrew J. Schmutzer and David M. Howard Jr. (Chicago: Moody, 2013), 52.

5 Paul Westermeyer, *Let Justice Sing: Hymnody and Justice* (Collegeville, MN: Liturgical Press, 1998), 28.

6 Ambrose of Milan, ca. 340–397, quoted in *A Sourcebook about Liturgy*, ed. Gabe Huck (Chicago: Liturgy Training Publications, 1994), 32–33.

The psalms also invite us to marvel at God's gift of creation: of mountains and hills, of fruit and cedar trees, of wild beasts and cattle, creeping things and flying birds (Ps. 148:9-10), and of earthquakes, lightning, roaring seas, and rivers that clap their hands (Ps. 29:7-8, Ps. 98:7-8). Fragments of psalms are part of our secular lexicon; even those who claim no religious affiliation are probably aware that "the Lord is my shepherd" is a psalm quotation. Home decor stores sell wall hangings emblazoned with single verses; other verses adorn national landmarks such as the Lincoln Memorial (Ps. 19:9) and the Library of Congress (Ps. 19:1).

Psalm texts abound in imagery and metaphor and can be adapted to suit virtually any context or format—indoor, outdoor, printed, paperless, stationary, mobile. They can be rendered by the smallest or largest of assemblies with the most economical or resplendent of musical means. Through repetition across the cycles and seasons of the church year, their language and wisdom enter memory. They strengthen and support us as we continue to sing the Lord's song in a strange land that is numbed, paralyzed, angry, and divided by violence, racism, misogyny, xenophobia, and so many other forms of prejudice. The psalms offer assurance and comfort to those affected by natural disasters, those who are exiled, and all who hang their harps and weep.

Accordingly, the psalms are indispensable texts for worshiping assemblies, and pastors and musicians should endeavor to sing the appointed psalm at each liturgy, even if chanted on a single tone. Unaccompanied chanting, in particular, allows an assembly to develop its voice by learning to breathe and listen together. For assemblies or leaders who may be new to psalm singing, or for those seeking to expand their repertoire of options, the following paragraphs offer a brief introduction to singing the psalms in worship.

Lutheran assemblies are accustomed to singing single- and double-tone formulas of eight and sixteen notes, respectively, a practice that became widespread following the publication of *Lutheran Book of Worship*. Its ten psalm-tone formulas were provided so that assemblies—not just soloists and choirs—could chant the psalms. The formatting of psalm texts for singing is called *pointing*. In *Evangelical Lutheran Worship*, a little superscript bar (|) shows where the psalm tone moves from the main note (called the *reciting tone*) to a short pattern of changing pitches (called the *cadence*). In addition to the many psalm tones printed in the pew editions of *Lutheran Book of Worship* (pp. 290–291), *Libro de Liturgia y Cántico* (p. 179), and *Evangelical Lutheran Worship* (pp. 337–338), many cantors compose their own psalm tones that, over time, become part of their assembly's musical fabric.

Although the entire assembly can chant a psalm from beginning to end, psalm verses can also be sung *antiphonally*—that is, by two groups in alternation. Antiphonal practice can take many forms depending on space, seating arrangement, availability of choirs or cantors, and the nature of a given service. Common forms of antiphonal singing utilize contrasting pairs such as left and right sides, choir and assembly, or cantor and assembly. Alternation is also dependent on the structure of the psalm itself: many assemblies sing whole verses in alternation. In the case of double tones, they alternate by pairs of verses. Attentive leaders also consider the ways in which halves of verses suggest ideas for antiphonal singing. This important aspect of Hebrew poetry, called *parallelism*, can appear in a psalm as:

Synonymous parallelism
Two halves of a verse repeat similar ideas
> The LORD is my light and my salvation;
> whom then | shall I fear?
> The LORD is the stronghold of my life;
> of whom shall I | be afraid?
> —Psalm 27:1

Contrasting parallelism
Two halves of a verse present contrasting ideas
> Some trust in chariots and | some in horses,
> but we rely on the name of the | LORD our God.
> —Psalm 20:7

Synthetic parallelism
An idea from the first half is expanded in the second half
> Blow the ram's horn at | the new moon,
> and at the full moon, the day | of our feast.
> —Psalm 81:3

Stepped parallelism

A refrain is used to fortify a succession of ideas

> Give thanks to the LORD, for the | LORD is good,
> for God's mercy en- | dures forever.
> Give thanks to the | God of gods,
> for God's mercy en- | dures forever.
> Give thanks to the | Lord of lords,
> for God's mercy en- | dures forever.
> —Psalm 136:1-3

The gamut of imagery and emotions expressed in the psalms and their poetic structures invites diverse possibilities of interpretation and accompaniment. The organ's ability to sustain pitch makes it ideal for accompanying psalmody, or at least introducing psalm tones if the verses are to be chanted a cappella. Yet psalm tones can also be introduced or accompanied by virtually any instrument. To counter the natural decay of tone, pianists can support the chanting of psalms by rolling chords of the tone and rearticulating when there is a natural break in the text, usually indicated by punctuation. Handbells can also provide a harmonic nest for the chanting of psalms. A chord—one that supplies pitch and signals breath—can be struck between each verse, and the singing bell technique can be used throughout the psalm to sustain important pitches.

Psalms can also employ refrains, a practice known as responsorial psalmody; the refrain acts as a response to the verses. Sometimes referred to as antiphons, refrains often consist of a verse, an excerpt of a verse, or a paraphrase of a few verses that emphasize a central theme of the psalm or an idea that relates to the day's other readings. In *Evangelical Lutheran Worship*, verse numbers of refrains are shown in red type after the psalm listings throughout the Propers section at the front of the book (pp. 18–63). Refrains may bookend the psalm verses and sometimes be inserted into the psalm itself, perhaps at key structural points—when verses can be divided into equal halves, thirds, and so forth—or at moments in the text where it makes sense to reiterate the central idea. Like the chanting of psalm verses, refrains can take many forms depending on context, and several model collections are listed at the end of this chapter. In addition to the wealth of printed settings, many cantors fashion their own refrains as part of their spiritual discipline or as a means of practicing the craft of composition (just as one practices the crafts of playing, singing, conducting, and leading other forms of assembly song). If you know that the children's choir, handbells, and a flautist will be available for the same service, compose or arrange a refrain that allows the full ensemble to help lead assembly singing.

Refrains can also be hewn from hymn stanzas; consider singing the first line of "Many and great, O God" (ELW 837) as a refrain for Psalm 8 or "Praise, praise, praise the Lord!" (ELW 875) with Psalm 148 or Psalm 150. Hymnal companions and scripture concordances are particularly useful for matching hymns to psalm texts. In addition to hymns, many shorter songs from the Taizé and Iona traditions are based on psalm verses, are adaptations of psalm verses, or are intended to frame the singing of psalms. These short ostinato pieces can also function as refrains; however, leaders will want to carefully consider the appropriateness of psalm refrains that have been adapted to reflect Christological themes. Refrains can also be excerpted from the deep well of psalm-based choral repertoire, a practice that allows smaller choirs to sing portions or adaptations of works that may otherwise be beyond their means or ability.

And yet not all psalms need refrains. During more restrained seasons such as Advent and Lent, a simple rendering of the psalm verses—perhaps a cappella—can be far more effective than an ornate antiphon and tone. However, throughout the twelve days of Christmas and the fifty days of Easter, more resplendent psalmody is certainly appropriate for "keeping festival" (Ps. 42:4).

The church's treasury of assembly song also includes a large number of metrical and through-composed psalm settings, such as "O God, our help in ages past" (ELW 632, after Psalm 90), as well as Christological hymns by Martin Luther built on ideas from psalms, such as "A mighty fortress is our God" (ELW 503–505, after Psalm 46) and "Out of the depths I cry to you" (ELW 600, after Psalm 130). For assemblies still developing the confidence to chant psalms, leaders may find it useful to explore the versifications and metrical translations listed under "Psalm Paraphrases" in *Indexes to Evangelical*

Lutheran Worship (p. 266). In addition, psalm resources for the assembly can also be adapted from Eastern Orthodox chant, early American music, spirituals, gospel and jazz idioms, and a panoply of global styles. The resource *Psalms for All Seasons* listed at the end of this chapter offers a wonderful compendium of ideas.

There is no shortage of options or creativity for singing the psalms in worship. But more important than how we sing the psalms is *that* we aspire to sing them in the first place. Our assemblies deserve the opportunity to give voice to these important and timeless texts, to let their words and wisdom seep into memory through regular use in worship, to have their chanting supported by thoughtful and well-crafted settings that enliven their vividness and immediacy. We sing the psalms, just as the psalmists themselves have instructed: "Hallelujah! Sing to the Lord a new song, God's praise in the assembly of the faithful" (Ps. 149:1).

Music during communion

Singing has always surrounded the eucharistic meal: According to Matthew and Mark, after the last supper, Jesus and the disciples sang a hymn before going to the Mount of Olives (Matt. 26:30, Mark 14:26). At their meal gatherings in homes and, eventually, in churches, early Christians also sang together. As *Principles for Worship* affirms,

> Music surrounds and serves the
> celebration of the sacraments. As part
> of God's creation renewed in Christ, the
> people of God sing around the elements,
> words, and actions that bear God's grace.[7]

Like many liturgical practices, use of music during communion varies considerably according to context. A community's particular ability, physical space, and piety all inform choices about singing around the table. Within their contexts, pastors and cantors should consider the richness of variety, practice, and possibility through the rhythms and seasons of the church year, maintaining focus on the assembly and its collective voice.

Particular attention might first be given to where and how the Agnus Dei ("Lamb of God") may be sung. In the medieval church this text was chanted as the bread was broken and the elements prepared for distribution. After the Reformation some Lutheran congregations sang it at the conclusion of the distribution. Today the practice is more varied. In some places the assembly remains standing to sing the Lamb of God after the invitation to the table while communion ministers take their places. Other assemblies sing it as the first communion song, though the various movements of the assembly—some approaching the table, others watching the action unfold—can easily fragment the assembly's voice to the extent that the Lamb of God is sung poorly, perhaps not at all. Care should be taken

7   *Principles for Worship,* 34.

to avoid moments like this that adversely affect the assembly's voice and its confidence.

Planners should also consider an appropriate balance between sound and silence. Silence is an appropriate option for the most solemn days of the church year, such as Ash Wednesday and Sunday of the Passion. Silence may also be appropriate during Lent, or perhaps more silence than usual by singing a single hymn instead of planning for wall-to-wall sound during the entire meal. The rich treasury of assembly song—and its ability to connect to the actions and meaning of the meal, and to a given day's lectionary readings or a season—offers a number of options for deepening focus and equipping God's people with texts and tunes to sing their faith. Some texts can relate to the day's lectionary, while others foster contemplation of communion itself. Still others can give thanks for the gifts of creation—wheat, grapes, harvesting hands, bakers, grocers, and more—that provide physical materials for the sharing of bread and wine. Singing during the meal can also be shaped by the seasons of the church year. For instance, here are some possible seasonal patterns:

Advent

- Begin distribution on each of the four Sundays with a seasonally appropriate Taizé chant such as "Wait for the Lord" (ELW 262); repetition across multiple Sundays helps commit this song to memory, and children should be encouraged to sing it at home with their families (perhaps while lighting the candles of a home Advent wreath).

- Follow this chant with a shorter, lectionary-appropriate hymn.
- Conclude distribution with a short, seasonally appropriate hymn such as "He came down" (ELW 253).

Time after Epiphany

- Sing "Jesus, come! for we invite you" (ELW 312) each Sunday of the season.
- Follow the hymn with a quiet instrumental offering or improvisation.
- Conclude with one of many Taizé chants or shorter songs—a different one each week—that focuses on the season's images of light.

Lent

- Sing a longer trope (variant) of the Agnus Dei such as "Lamb of God, pure and sinless" (ELW 357) as the first distribution hymn.
- Follow the Agnus Dei with a plainsong or a cappella hymn such as "Thee we adore, O Savior" (ELW 476) that sonically reflects the austerity of the season and worship space.
- Let the remainder of the distribution conclude in silence.

Easter

- Begin distribution with one of many Taizé chants or shorter songs—a different one each week or perhaps "Be not afraid" (ELW 388) each Sunday—that shout "alleluia" and help the assembly keep festival during the full, fifty-day Easter season.
- Then sing a longer, lectionary-appropriate hymn.

Summer

- Begin the distribution in silence or with instrumental music.
- Then, when most worshipers have returned to their places, a cantor may teach or lead a paperless song; perhaps the assembly can learn three or four of these songs throughout the summer, then subsequently use them (planned or unplanned) for worship, meetings, devotions, or grace before meals.

Because of the physical movements associated with distribution—the difficulties of holding a hymnal while receiving bread or singing while drinking from a chalice—the meal is rarely the time to introduce new or unfamiliar melodies. The advice given in *The Sunday Assembly* is worth repeating in full:

> For all these reasons, selecting music that will continue even when only a portion of the assembly is singing is important. Choosing simple songs during communion allows the assembly to join in as they wait in line to commune, to pray, or to silently listen as they commune. In some assemblies, worshipers may even take printed communion songs with them to the table. In any case, planners should make choices that will allow the song to continue during this flexible and open time.

A further consideration here is the potential to develop and choose song that doesn't depend on having a service folder or book in hand. Memorized songs allow an assembly to continue singing during communion and eliminates the need to use the service folder or worship book to sing, allowing the assembly to focus more on the song itself. It also encourages the assembly to develop and expand its memory.[8]

Pastors and musicians should also plan for instances when several stanzas of a longer hymn remain once distribution has ended. Should the hymn be brought to a close, or should the arc of the stanzas' poetry be allowed to conclude? Most assemblies will find it jarring to conclude "Brightest and best of the stars" (ELW 303) at stanza 3 with a question mark or to end "Let all mortal flesh keep silence" (ELW 490) without singing "alleluia" with the seraphim and cherubim in stanza 4. Care should also be taken to decide (usually in advance) about how cantors and choirs can participate in the meal without disrupting their leadership of the assembly's singing.

Regardless of context, each and every choice about what to sing and how to sing it—from the longest hymn of the day to the shortest communion song—should sprout from a desire to sustain and nurture the voice of the gathered assembly. Like Christ's body broken and shared at eucharistic tables, assembly song is also broken and shared for the sake of the world. Texts and melodies are ordinary things with extraordinary properties. Like bread and wine, even small morsels of song—short refrains or snippets of longer hymns—can nourish, sustain,

8 Lorraine S. Brugh and Gordon W. Lathrop, *The Sunday Assembly* (Minneapolis: Augsburg Fortress, 2008), 220.

and form us to be that singing, serving, and praying body of Christ in the world. Or, as Susan Palo Cherwien has written for us to sing:

> God, may our hearts be grateful,
> And may our words be true.
> May all our songs be noble
> And draw us deep in you,
> That singing holy stories,
> More holy we become,
> Transposed into like spirits
> To be your loving home.[9]

9 Susan Palo Cherwien, "What Joyous Song Unfolding," stanza 4, in *Peace, Be Still* (Minneapolis: Augsburg Fortress, 2017), 53.

Resources

Books

- Brueggemann, Walter, and William H. Bellinger Jr. *Psalms* (New Cambridge Bible Commentary). Cambridge and New York: Cambridge University Press, 2014.
- Lamport, Mark A., Benjamin K. Forrest, and Vernon M. Whaley, eds. *Hymns and Hymnody: Historical and Theological Introductions*, 3 vols. Eugene, OR: Cascade Books, 2019.
- McLean, Terri Brocklund, and Rob Glover. *Choosing Contemporary Music: Seasonal, Topical, Lectionary Indexes*. Minneapolis: Augsburg Fortress, 2000.
- Mueller, Craig. *Indexes to Evangelical Lutheran Worship*. Minneapolis: Augsburg Fortress, 2007.
- Ramshaw, Gail. *Treasures Old and New: Images in the Lectionary*. Minneapolis: Fortress Press, 2002.
- Torvend, Samuel. *Still Hungry at the Feast: Eucharistic Justice in the Midst of Affliction*. Collegeville, MN: Liturgical Press, 2019.
- Witvliet, John D. *The Biblical Psalms in Christian Worship: A Brief Introduction and Guide to Resources*. Grand Rapids, MI: William B. Eerdmans, 2007.

Taizé and Iona collections (GIA Publications, Inc.)

- https://www.giamusic.com/sacred_music/resourcepage_taize.cfm
- https://www.giamusic.com/sacred_music/resourcepage_iona.cfm

Psalm collections (Augsburg Fortress)

- *Psalter for Worship,* 3 volumes. Minneapolis: Augsburg Fortress, 2006–2008.
- *Psalm Settings for the Church Year: Revised Common Lectionary.* Minneapolis: Augsburg Fortress, 2008.
- *ChildrenSing Psalms.* Minneapolis: Augsburg Fortress, 2009.

Psalm collections (other publishers)

- Hallock, Peter R. *The Ionian Psalter.* Honolulu: Ionian Arts, Inc., 2007, https://ionianarts.com/the-ionian-psalter/
- Litton, James, ed. *The Plainsong Psalter.* New York: Church Publishing, 1988.
- Tel, Martin, ed. *Psalms for All Seasons: A Complete Psalter for Worship.* Grand Rapids, MI: Faith Alive Christian Resources, 2012.

Leading 3 assembly song

They ministered with song … and they
performed their service in due order.
—1 Chronicles 6:32

To lead a singing assembly is an extraordinary feat of multitasking: one simultaneously leads, accompanies, follows, adapts, proclaims, preaches, interprets, performs, listens, orchestrates, and much more. As Paul Westermeyer has observed, to lead well is to eventually become unnecessary. During just one hymn or over the span of several services, a capable leader helps the assembly to recognize and cherish its own, distinct voice. Musicians may offer guideposts (when to breathe, when to sing) and supporting frameworks (rhythm, harmony), but their work always yields to the primary musical instrument: the voice of the gathered assembly.

Preparing to lead

The Lutheran cantor Paul Manz once remarked to a group of organists that "I can never know the hymns too well." How true for any church musician! The leadership of assembly song—of knowing these songs well, even *too* well—begins with thoughtful study of text, even reading the text aloud away from the keyboard. One may ask, for example:

- What are these stanzas about?
- Who is doing what for whom? Why?
- Do any stanzas differ in character or sentiment from the others? If so, might they be rendered in ways that draw attention to their texts? For example:

"Forgive our sins as we forgive" (ELW 605) begins with a quotation from the Lord's Prayer. Perhaps a keyboardist could play the phrases set off by quotation marks in unison at a *forte* (strong) dynamic.

Notice, too, the quotations in the first half of each stanza of "I heard the voice of Jesus say" (ELW 611). Perhaps an organist can play these phrases with a solo stop such as a trumpet in the treble or tenor register.

Or consider the gradual crescendo of images in "Abide with me" (ELW 629), from the deepening darkness of dusk (stanza 1) to the fleeing of shadows as heaven's morning breaks (stanza 5). What an occasion for a matching musical crescendo!

The list of considerations for preparing to lead assembly song continues:

- When and where will this be sung? What is the liturgical context? Cultural context? What do these words have the power to do in this time and place?
- Where are the syllabic stresses? Important nouns? Active verbs? Notable metaphors? Important punctuation?

These questions and others like them assist cantors in making musical decisions about the text—its heartbeat, its most vivid images, its challenges—before a single note is played.

Principles for leading

Regardless of style, instrument, or space—and whether composed in the 1690s or the 1960s—a few core principles transcend leadership decisions for virtually any style of assembly song.

Tactus, timing, breath

A *tactus* is the pulse or rhythm of a hymn or song. Sometimes the tactus is the same as the beat, but it often encompasses two or more beats. Sing the first line of the hymn "Love divine, all loves excelling" (ELW 631). Although this hymn has three quarter-note beats per measure, it can be *felt* in dotted half-note pulses: those dotted half-note pulses are the tactus, and each pulse of the tactus matches strong syllables in the text:

Love div**ine** all **loves** exc**el**ling

Or consider the hymn "Joyful, joyful we adore thee" (ELW 836). There are four quarter notes per measure, but the tactus can often be assigned to the half note, even the whole note:

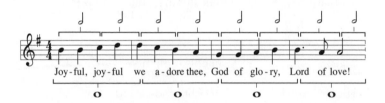

Joyful, **joy**ful **we** a**dore** thee, **God** of **glo**ry, **Lord** of **love**!
Joyful, joyful **we** adore thee, **God** of glory, **Lord** of love!

In other styles, however, the tactus is not evenly divided into groups of two, three, or four beats. Chantlike melodies are often organized into pulses of two- and three-note groups such as this example from "Glory to God" (ELW 162):

Alternating two- and three-note patterns are also a hallmark of rhythmic Renaissance tunes such as Freu dich sehr, shown here with implied time signatures for the beginning of the hymn "Signs and wonders" (ELW 672):

Underlying dance rhythms in hymns and their accompaniments are usually a good indicator of tactus. Examples include:

Dance or Rhythm	Tactus	Example(s)
Calypso	Half note	"The right hand of God" (ELW 889)
Corrido	Quarter note	"The Lord now sends us forth" (ELW 538)
Habanera	Quarter note	"We plow the fields and scatter" (ELW 680)
Waltz	Dotted half note	"Alleluia! Jesus is risen!" (ELW 377) "Silent night, holy night" (ELW 281) "The peace of the Lord" (ELW 646)

The *Musicians Guide to Evangelical Lutheran Worship* provides tactus and other leadership suggestions for each hymn, and the pew edition of *Libro de Liturgia y Cántico* (pp. 627–639) provides a rhythmic index for dance styles that both infuse and propel hymns of Latin American origin: some of these are also discussed in the *Musicians Guide* (pp. 66–67).

As part of their personal preparation, skilled cantors read texts aloud in ways that help them sense the flow of vowels, consonants, and syllabic stresses within the meter and tactus. Practice time for reading and singing texts is needed before practice time at one's instrument: the agility of a pianist's fingers or an organist's feet are not always good barometers for the agility of the intricate human vocal mechanism. Even if a lively tune wants to dance, a tempo that is too brisk makes it difficult to sing the text. In what may now be a familiar refrain in this book, decisions about tactus and tempo depend on contextual questions such as:

- When and where will this hymn be sung?
- What bearing does the time of day or placement in the service have on tactus?
- What are the acoustics of the worship space?
- What instrument(s) will lead the singing?
- How are considerations of tactus translated into specific techniques for these instruments?

Breath

Once a tactus begins, it continues steadily throughout the entire duration of the hymn. Rests for breathing at punctuation and timing between stanzas should fit within the tactus, not be inserted in ways that add beats or distort its pulse. For example, a half note at the end of a phrase should be shortened to a quarter note or dotted quarter note followed by a quarter rest or eighth rest for breath. The amount of time subtracted from the printed note value will depend on factors such as the pulse, acoustics, size of the assembly, and instruments. In any case, do not hold the half note for full value, then upset the meter by adding value for the breath:

"Come, thou Fount of every blessing" (ELW 807)

In his book *Let the People Sing*, David Cherwien describes an "all hands off" approach to the timing between hymn stanzas.[1] This is a two-step process, a stimulus and response; a lift—all hands (and feet) off the keyboard—is the cue for the assembly to breathe:

"Holy God, we praise your name" (ELW 414)

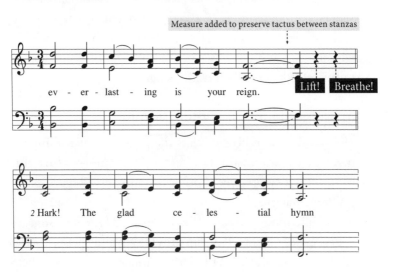

In addition to *Let the People Sing* (pp. 14–15), advice for the timing between stanzas is also provided in the aforementioned *Musicians Guide* (pages 42–43) as well as in *Leading the Church's Song* (pp. 48–49).

1 David M. Cherwien, *Let the People Sing: A Keyboardist's Creative and Practical Guide to Engaging God's People in Meaningful Song* (St. Louis: Concordia Publishing House, 1997), 14–15.

Introductions

Introductions can also take many forms, from extended impro-
visations inspired by images in the text to shorter, published
works. Good introductions not only prepare the assembly to sing,
but inspire a *want* to sing. No matter their length or complexity,
introductions should establish the key and tactus of the hymn
or song that follows, and there should be a clear distinction—
signaled through timing or a change in dynamic—between the
end of the introduction and the onset of the assembly's voice. The
all-hands-off technique used between stanzas of hymns applies
to any introduction: lift, breathe, sing!

Instruments, timbre, interpretation

Though the assembly's voice is the primary musical instrument in worship, cantors often support and nurture this
voice with a symphony of other instruments. Regardless of
instrumentation, accompaniments must be offered with confidence, intention, and care. The editors for *Musicians Guide to
Evangelical Lutheran Worship* provide a simple yet profound
guide when they ask: "Will this instrumentation serve to help
support the assembly in their corporate song?"[2]

Accompaniments and all that they encompass—tactus, tempo,
technique, timbre, and the like—must both lead and support,
often interchangeably. Accompaniments must also be planned
and practiced with text and context in mind; we want to dance

---

2   *Musicians Guide to Evangelical Lutheran Worship,* 26.

Easter "alleluias," but assemblies should not have to outshout the organ or band during a quiet evening hymn.

Thoughtful accompanists should strive to know as much as they can about the basic physiology of the human voice—particularly ways in which vowels and consonants are articulated—so that they can provide supportive and inspiring (*inspirare*, to "breathe into") accompaniments. A keyboardist's increased attention to their own diction, for example, can foster more nuanced articulation, such as varying degrees of stress and separation for syllables that begin with plosive consonants ("All **p**eople that on earth **d**o **d**well"); for rearticulated vowels ("Abide with me, fast fails th**e e**ventide"); for crisp movements of lips, teeth, and tongue ("Sen**t f**orth by Go**d's b**lessing"); and for the various types of punctuation and poetic techniques used by poets and translators. Note the use of punctuation in the following hymn stanza:

> How can any praise we offer measure all the thanks we owe?
> Take our hearts and hands and voices—
> gifts of love we can bestow.
> Alleluia! Alleluia! Triune God, to you we sing![3]

Accompanists must also remember that assembly song is notated for voices, not their respective instruments. Accompaniments must be made idiomatic for the instruments that play them. Organists who play in reverberant rooms may play in a more detached style, while pianists often adapt accompaniments with

3   Herman G. Stuempfle Jr., "Voices raised to you," in *Evangelical Lutheran Worship*, #845. Text © 1997, GIA Publications. Used by permission.

arpeggiated chords and "fill" gestures to counter the natural decay of tone after a note is struck.

Organists who "orchestrate" their instruments to serve assembly song should consider a balance of tones and colors that support (low, 16' and below), reinforce (unison, 8'), and lead (high, 4' and above).[4] Likewise, pianists should consider when it is helpful to assist the assembly by playing a melody an octave higher than written or by doubling the bass an octave below. And while most organs stand in fixed locations, pianos should be positioned in ways that best lead assembly song. For grand pianos, the long (bass) edge is best placed parallel to a sound-reflecting wall, the lid opened perpendicularly toward the assembly. Care should be taken to avoid placing pianos too close to windows or air vents, or in other locations that subject their intricate mechanics to damage caused by extreme fluctuations in temperature and humidity. Acoustic guitars can provide both harmonic and rhythmic reinforcement, and various percussion instruments can provide rhythmic layers for hymns and songs of many styles, especially those from traditions (such as music from the African continent or Latin America) where rhythmic counterpoint is a hallmark of musical expression.

In his writings, the twentieth-century French composer Olivier Messiaen often described how, in his mind, certain keys carried specific theological associations: E major often represented the praise of God, while F-sharp major often represented Christly

---

4   This threefold approach to organ registration—support, reinforce, lead—was developed by Daniel Schwandt for workshops on leading assembly song, and is described here with permission.

love. Similar musical-theological relationships have been explored in the works of other composers, such as J. S. Bach's use of rhythm, meter, and proportion. Although the intricacies of these topics are better suited to academic conferences populated by music theorists and music historians, many cantors—sometimes unconsciously, sometimes intentionally—employ similar techniques, developing a personal theology of sound that informs their leadership of assembly singing.

For example, an organist leading a hymn about love, peace, or humility might use warm colors such as 8' and 4' principals and strings along with gently voiced reeds such as an 8' clarinet. Perhaps a stanza about brightness or light calls for higher-pitched stops, the brilliance of mixtures, or a sparkling "gap" registration such as 8' and 2' (or 8' with 4' and 1⅓'). Pianists might approach the same text by momentarily shifting the right hand or both hands up an octave. Texts that mention depth or even thunder and lightning might be enlivened with the judicious use of 32' colors in the pedal, and chorus reeds—trumpets, clarions, and trombones—are effective for conveying a sense of power, majesty, and might. Phrases that emphasize unity, such as "We all are one in mission" (ELW 576), can be played in unison, while references to harmony such as "Help us to dwell in harmony and serve each other willingly" (ELW 746, st. 2) may offer occasion for the assembly to sing a cappella in parts.

Timbres provided through instrumental arrangements and descants can also be used to enhance the meaning of texts.

Stringed instruments, flutes, oboes, and clarinets can provide lyrical warmth, while brass instruments can add both power and brilliance to the leadership of assembly song. Of course, a trumpet can also be lyrical, while oboes and violins can add brilliance; context is key! Cantors should familiarize themselves with the ranges and capabilities of instruments available in their setting, as well as with ways instrumental parts may be adapted for common versions of transposing instruments such as horns (in F), trumpets and clarinets (in B♭), and alto saxophones (in E♭).

Just as good preachers prepare sermons by thinking about their goals before writing, cantors do well to consider their goals for a given hymn or song—a theological interpretation of its text or musical trajectory of its accompaniment—before practicing. And hymns must be practiced: not merely played through, but practiced—and ideally with a metronome!

A practiced hymn, one sensitive to text, context, musical mechanics—a steady tactus, clear indications for breathing, and a timbre sensitive to text—helps foster trust between cantor and assembly.

Choirs and assembly song

Ensembles of singers are a mainstay of scripture: Moses and the Israelites sang at the Red Sea (Exod. 15); duties of singers are described in temple stories (1 Chron., 2 Chron., Ezra); and Jesus and the disciples sang a hymn (Matt. 26:30, Mark 14:26) at the last supper. And, lest we forget, there are choirs of angels (Luke 2:13-14) and of morning stars (Job 38:7) too!

The principal role of a choir—whether a large ensemble that can easily sing in eight parts or an occasional group of volunteers who work tirelessly on a unison anthem—is to assist the assembly in its singing. For example:

- Choirs can help introduce and teach unfamiliar hymns.
- Choir members can be strategically placed in the assembly to help strengthen its singing, especially when a new liturgical setting is introduced, when the assembly is asked to process while singing, or at services where low attendance is expected.
- Choir members can be taught to use rhythm instruments for hymns and songs based on dance styles.
- The choir can regularly participate in weekly psalmody by chanting verses in alternation with the assembly or by singing a choral refrain.
- The choir can enrich any hymn with a well-crafted stanza setting or descant, or by singing a stanza in a different language.

> The choir's ability to lead is more important than its ability to perform.

Weekly anthems are not requirements, though many cantors still feel pressure to comply with this culturally conditioned commandment. Recently, a blog post from the Center for Congregational Song encouraged recasting these anxieties into new ideas that better serve the assembly. For example, instead of thinking, "We should sing an anthem each week," try thinking, "Each week, we help the assembly to sing better." Or, rather than "We're nervous about this piece, but we have to sing it," try "We now have the confidence to share this musical offering with the community" instead.[5]

Cantors who conduct choirs should prioritize the leadership of assembly song in their rehearsal planning and repertoire selection. Hymns can be incorporated into warm-up exercises, and their rehearsal invites practice of phrasing, blend, and vowel production based on sensitive reading of text. Strong choral support also helps instrumentalists establish tactus and tempo, and helps guide the singing assembly through stanza assignments such as alternation between treble and lower voices or a cappella singing. The choir's participation in leading assembly song is never a secondary matter, nor should its role be left to chance.

The notion of the choir as an ensemble that serves the assembly is not meant to discount or dissuade ensembles of professionally trained singers that offer difficult works in the context of the liturgy. Like stained glass, a beautifully designed baptismal font, freshly baked bread, or visual art printed in a worship folder or projected on a screen, musical artistry serves both word and sacrament. But at a time when communal singing is rare, when professionally recorded and edited music is omnipresent, and when vocal ability has been commercialized through enterprises such as American Idol, our culture often signals to God's people

5   Brian Hehn, "A Pastor's Music Question," https://congregationalsong.org/a-pastors-music-question/, accessed September 1, 2019.

that they do not possess requisite talent for singing. Choirs that only perform repertoire at the offertory or whose amplification overpowers assembly singing can, unfortunately, reinforce the attitude that the singing of God's people is a specialized activity for a select few. Caution should also be exercised around choir-centric planning, such as a "cantata Sunday" or a "music Sunday." Though well-intended, such services unwittingly participate in the commercialization of music and worship, suggesting that music is to be displayed and consumed as a finished product rather than made together by a community.

The choir's offerings are part of the overall balance of styles, genres, and expressions for a given service. If a day's hymnody contains a disproportionate amount of music by Caucasian or northern European authors and composers, then the conscientious cantor may ask the choir to sing music by women, African American composers, or other historically marginalized communities. A conscientious cantor will think beyond the anthem or offertory and endeavor to imagine how the choir can surround, support, and enhance the assembly's voice. Sing at different places in the service and perhaps even different locations in the worship space. Sing among the people during processions. Sit among the people when new songs and liturgy settings are introduced. And though these paragraphs focus more on adult choirs, similar concepts apply to ensembles for children and youth of all ages. Thoughtful leaders attend not only to the musical training of young voices but also to their faith formation, a topic addressed in the next chapter.

Resources

Books

- Farlee, Robert Buckley, ed. *Leading the Church's Song*. Minneapolis: Augsburg Fortress, 1998.
- Folkening, John. *Handbells in the Liturgical Service*. St. Louis: Concordia Publishing House, 1984.
- Forster, Stuart. *Hymn Playing: A Modern Colloquium*. St. Louis: MorningStar Music Publishers, 2013.
- Parker, Alice. *Melodious Accord: Good Singing in Church*. Chicago: Liturgy Training Publications, 1991.
- Schalk, Carl F. *First Person Singular: Reflections on Worship, Liturgy, and Children*. St. Louis: MorningStar Music Publishers, 1998.
- Schmidt, Clayton J., ed. *A Teaching Hymnal: Ecumenical and Evangelical*. Eugene, OR: Wipf & Stock, 2018.
- Zager, Daniel, and Steven Wente. *The Choir and the Organ in Early Lutheranism*. Minneapolis: Lutheran University Press, 2017.

Choral resources

- *Augsburg Chorale Book*. Minneapolis: Augsburg Fortress, 2017.
- *Bach for All Seasons*. Minneapolis: Augsburg Fortress, 1999.
- *Chantry Choirbook: Sacred Music for All Seasons*. Minneapolis: Augsburg Fortress, 2000.
- *Choral Stanzas for Hymns*, 2 vols. Minneapolis: Augsburg Fortress, 2010–2011.
- *GladSong Choirbook: Contemporary Music for the Church Year*. Minneapolis: Augsburg Fortress, 2005.
- *Sing the Stories of God's People: Thirty More Songs for the Youngest Singers*. Minneapolis: Augsburg Fortress, 2010.

Treasure, too, you have entrusted,
gain through pow'rs your grace conferred;
ours to use for home and kindred,
and to spread the gospel word.
Open wide our hands in sharing,
as we heed Christ's ageless call,
healing, teaching, and reclaiming,
serving you by loving all.

"God, whose giving knows no ending"
Evangelical Lutheran Worship, #678

Cantors and community

So far, this book has discussed the work of church musicians through the lens of selecting and leading assembly song. This is, of course, the most important task of the cantor, keyboardist, choir director, band leader, director of music, minister of music, director of worship, or any title by which church musicians are known in their respective contexts. To select and lead assembly song is a fundamentally collaborative endeavor. Planning entails consideration of the assembly and other musicians, as well as consultation with pastors and other leaders. Singing necessitates listening, cooperation, and adaptation. The work of church musicians thus requires collaborators—literally, "co-laborers"—in the community. Likewise, church musicians are co-laborers in other ministries of the congregation and the wider church; all work together, and a rich harmony arises from this counterpoint.

Although the roles of church musicians are shaped by the physical materials of their music making—hymnals, other printed music, reference resources, instruments, and the like—equally important are ways in which their personal and professional relationships support the singing of God's people. The purpose of this chapter is not to prescribe rules and regulations for behavior and comportment; no single model can account for the boundless variety of gifts, personalities, and working styles of church musicians in their respective contexts. Rather, these paragraphs invite further reflection about what it means to truly *attend* to—literally, "to stretch toward"—one's community as part of one's vocation.

Relinquishing musical power

Cantors must first recognize that, whether desired or not, they possess power in their communities. This power takes many forms and expressions, among them: the physiological power of sound, the emotional power of musical expression and memory, the power that accompanies visibility and responsibility in leadership roles, and the power to form and shape faith. This is not a recent development. Stories of music's power are recorded in scripture, and the power attributed to both music and musicians has been the subject of ardent debate since the earliest days of the church: David played the lyre to soothe Saul (1 Sam. 16:23); God admonished those who would make music in worship solely for their own edification (Amos 5:23-24); ancient Greek philosophers debated music's influence on character and development; and Augustine worried that the emotional power of music could eclipse reason, that sensation could overwhelm intellect. As music historian Christopher Page has observed, even a fourth-century meeting of bishops reflected tensions about the power of music and its practitioners. Records of their discussions, he writes, "sound the note that becomes so familiar as the centuries pass: singers are necessary for the celebration of the liturgy but are constantly to be kept under surveillance."[1]

For most church musicians, realization or acknowledgment of their power is uncomfortable, if not downright terrifying; their sense of vocation is rooted in commitment to service, not visions of celebrity. But to cultivate good, honest, and trustworthy relationships in their communities, musicians should foster awareness of how their roles are perceived by staff colleagues, choir members, children, and the assembly. This awareness is not an excuse for musicians to harness or wield power for selfish purposes but, instead, to encourage reflection about how that power can be relinquished or redirected in the service of others. As Mark Tranvik has observed, "A sense of calling has the possibility of transforming power from an ethic of domination to an ethic of service."[2] Likewise, in an essay titled "Musical Power: Broken to the Center," Lutheran cantor and composer Mark Mummert tells us:

> Whenever any power is brought to a Christian assembly, we must consider what we will do with such power. Like the powers of privilege that come from class, rank, gender, wealth, or

1   Christopher Page, *The Christian West and Its Singers: The First Thousand Years* (New Haven and London: Yale University Press, 2010), 90.

2   *Martin Luther and the Called Life*, 162.

> status, musical power must always yield to the
> purpose of the assembly. In fact, in a Christian
> assembly, power is wielded in the way Christ
> himself is powerful—by being broken.[3]

How, then, do cantors break open power in order to form deep, meaningful relationships with communities they serve? There is, of course, no easy answer. For some, hospitality and grace seem intrinsic, natural gifts that convey a sense of approachability and openness to conversation about all manner of topics. For some (such as me, a bookish introvert), enormous reserves of stamina must be summoned to have even the shortest of conversations following the postlude. Whether introverted or extroverted, cantors who participate in fellowship opportunities with their assemblies—who exude joy, enthusiasm, thoughtfulness in their work—ultimately do more to dismantle perceptions of musical power than those who bolt for the nearest exit after a flawless performance of service music. Some cantors build community relationships through teaching, some through their work with children, and some through the offerings of a congregational arts series. Regardless of their gifts, personalities, or working methods, most church musicians instinctively understand that to stretch beyond their personal comfort zones is to resist temptations that accompany musical power and privilege. This also affords vocational encouragement, a reminder that assemblies are always listening, observing, feeling, and thinking. Even on

---

3 Mark Mummert, "Musical Power: Broken to the Center," in *Centripetal Worship: The Evangelical Heart of Lutheran Worship*, ed. Timothy J. Wengert (Minneapolis: Augsburg Fortress, 2007), 39.

the days that seem mundane or perhaps inadequate—when the hymns didn't seem to fit quite right, when the spacing between two stanzas of the hymn of the day was botched, or when things just felt lackluster—a sibling in Christ may describe their experience of something heard, sung, or spoken that offered them comfort, insight, assurance, or hope.

In *Church Musicians: Reflections on Their Call, Craft, History, and Challenges*, Paul Westermeyer frames the relational aspects of a church musician's vocation through an important question that orients the power of music and musicians toward the singing of God's people. How, he asks, might we best "attend to ethnic, linguistic, sociological, psychological, musicological, [and] ethnomusicological characteristics of our respective communities?"[4] Here, Westermeyer invokes the discipline of ethnomusicology, the study of how music functions in culture. As part of their fieldwork, ethnomusicologists engage in observing, recording, establishing and maintaining relationships, and navigating ethical questions posed by their dual status as both outsider (visitor) and insider (member). Like ethnomusicologists, church musicians live, move, and have their being across a variety of liminal, in-between spaces such as servant and leader, doer and observer, employee and member. This is not unlike the paradox of music itself, observed by Martin Luther, namely that it is both queen and servant. As Samuel Torvend notes:

4   Paul Westermeyer, *Church Musicians: Reflections on Their Call, Craft, History, and Challenges* (St. Louis: MorningStar Music Publishers, 2015), 9.

> The key, of course, is that the ruler becomes the servant for the good of his people; the celebrity shakes off the need to hear the crowd's adulation and pours out his or her charisma for those in need; the one who possesses power does not impress with that power, but gives it away, shares it so that others have life ... or singing.[5]

As musicians and servants, cantors are to carry themselves with tact and grace in all forms of communication, musical or otherwise. This is not always easy, especially when fielding complaints. Yet difficult conversations provide opportunities for asking important questions that, in turn, deepen understanding of the assembly and its needs. Often, a complaint or criticism is an exterior symptom of a deeper question, feeling, or source of conflict that may be unrecognized by its source. Sometimes, lack of specialized technical language obscures meaning. Instead of observing that "the amplitude of the 8' trumpet on the organ makes it difficult to sing when it is drawn with the full principal chorus," a cantor may simply be told that "the organ is too loud." Rather than assuming a defensive posture, cantors can respond by politely asking for more information. For example: "Was there a particular place in the service where you noticed this?" "Would you say that the sound was too brassy and reedy, or was it too high-pitched?"

---

5   Samuel Torvend, "The Musician as Artist, Pastor, and Prophet: Rethinking Vocation in Troubled Times," *CrossAccent: Journal of the Association of Lutheran Church Musicians* 11.1 (Spring 2003), 12.

"Out of curiosity, where were you sitting?" Awareness of these factors—that high mixtures or bold trumpet stops sound louder in certain parts of the space—might help an organist encourage singing through more judicious registration rather than unknowingly continuing to hinder or silence voices that cannot compete with the instrument.

Follow-up questions are also important for comments such as "I didn't like that hymn" or "We don't sing this hymn enough." Perhaps it was not the hymn text or tune itself that was objectionable, but that the tempo was too slow or the introduction unclear. Or perhaps a difficult interval or other counterintuitive passage could be taught in advance or assisted more purposefully with choral support, such as seating some or all of the choir among the assembly. Perhaps the deacon who wants to sing "Children of the heavenly father" (ELW 781) more often just sang that hymn at the funeral of a loved one. In these instances, it is usually more constructive to listen, pause, and ask clarifying questions rather than respond with technical babble about the physics of organ construction or the intricacies of lectionary-based service planning. Above all, cantors should express thanks and appreciation for these comments, and welcome the opportunity for conversation. A central premise of this book is that one must love the people more than the music. At times that can be enormously difficult, especially when one's hours of personal preparation, care, and thoughtfulness seem underappreciated. But this love for our assemblies is rooted in the breaking of power, and even complaints provide opportunities to better know the assemblies we serve, to learn how to empower the singing of all God's people.

Like pastors and other church leaders, the church musician's work is often solitary and hidden. Seldom do members of the assembly watch the pastor write a sermon or listen to the musician practice hymns and learn parts for a choral anthem. There are (usually) no witnesses when a sermon idea hatches while the pastor is jogging or when a musical idea flashes across the cantor's mind while shopping for groceries. Accordingly, musicians may find it beneficial to foster a sense of transparency and ownership about assembly song in their communities, to think in terms of sharing a process rather than simply displaying a finished result. Some do this by writing weekly worship-folder notes, social media posts about worship, or newsletter columns, or through an annual report for a congregational meeting. Other considerations include:

- Could members of the choir or assembly be invited to write some of these things?
- Could the cantor lead adult education sessions about the lectionary and songs for an upcoming liturgical season, or perhaps a forum about hymn selection?
- Is it worthwhile to discuss why some hymns or songs were *not* selected for a given service?
- Does the language used in conversation or writing show that the point of departure is the assembly's voice, not the musician's whims, training, tastes, or interests?

And for musicians who serve in spaces with apses, balconies, or other architectural features that prevent them from being seen, consider the significance of being visible—of communing at the table, of leading paperless music by rote, of reading a lesson, or of teaching a new song—in and among the assembly. To make eye contact, to sing a solo, to literally be on the same level as the assembly is important for building community.

> Attending to the assembly—breaking
> open the inherent power of music and
> the power ascribed (rightfully or not) to
> musicians—is a self-emptying act of
> which deep, heartfelt listening and
> open communication are key components.
> It's using one's gifts to enflesh and empower
> the voices that come together for worship.

This is not just an exercise for musicians: even the first chapter of a handbook for lectors gives sound advice that is useful for any leader: "Listen carefully!"[6]

Honoring vocation in the community

Cantors are also called to carefully consider ways they interact with choirs and staff colleagues—not only pastors, but also office administrators, sextons, assisting ministers, and all whose callings serve the needs of the gathered assembly.

6   Christopher George Hoyer, *Getting the Word Out: A Handbook for Readers* (Minneapolis: Augsburg Fortress, 2013), 15.

Cantors, choirs, and children

Choir rehearsals for singers of all ages provide opportunities not only for preparation of music that will help lead or augment assembly song, but also for faith formation. Like the selection of hymns, liturgical settings, and other attendant music, rehearsal planning can also be guided by careful consideration of one's context and of attending to the experiences and needs of the musicians who gather. Consider, for example:

Who are these singers, and why are they here?

If they wanted to sing difficult repertoire for applauding audiences, these singers would likely be elsewhere and not in a church choir. They may not have the same training or experiences as you or as singers in professional ensembles, but they, too, have answered the call of the Holy Spirit to share their divinely given gifts with others. They want to sing, and they want to serve—faithfully. While cantors and conductors naturally desire musical excellence, demands for perfection can quickly diminish this sense of community and desire to serve. A conscientious cantor will strive to hold these perspectives in balance, to be an encouraging and nurturing presence.

What are we singing about in rehearsals?

Some conductors begin rehearsal with prayer or reflection. This not only provides focus for the task at hand, but also offers a buffer from the hustle and bustle of the world—a chance to breathe and enter the sacred story of which they sing, to let go of the troubles that happened at work, the blaring of horns in traffic, the noise of the news. The music director at a congregation where I once served as an accompanist would often begin rehearsal with a reflection, either about the music to be practiced or about the readings for the next service. Sometimes the reflections were the director's own. Sometimes they came from existing resources like the *One-Minute Devotions for the Church Musician* series listed at the end of this chapter. In some places, choir members maintain a schedule that allows them to offer reflections too (remember, church musicians work to empower others and do not claim each and every task for themselves). After the reflection, the music director would, in these or similar words, ask: "For whom else or what else do we pray?" Together, we would listen. Together, we would pray. Together, we would remind ourselves that rehearsal was not only about notes, rhythms, vowel shapes, phrasing, and where to breathe, but also about God's people.

What is this text about?

Some choir directors find it helpful to have singers read portions of text aloud, a chance to hear how individual voices stress different words, inflect with pitch, and render the rhythms of syntax—all of which build crucial listening skills within ensembles. Drawing attention to such moments—or, again, leading a short devotion about ideas, images, or metaphors and their musical treatment—ultimately allows the music to become a more effective vehicle for text. When voices share a textual goal, musical cohesion often follows. The word *love* will sound lovely without the director having to explain how to sing it.

Choir directors will also want to carefully plan (and periodically evaluate) the structure of their rehearsals. Using a dry-erase board or paper and easel, conductors can indicate materials needed—octavos, printed song collections, paper copies of the psalm—as well as the rehearsal order. Such organization helps clarify goals and objectives for the ensemble and often promotes focus and teamwork. Rather than singing through each piece a few times, it is best to work on isolated, difficult sections first, then put them into the larger context of the piece. Advance preparation and score study not only help conductors anticipate challenges, but also suggest technical solutions—such as for a difficult interval or rhythm—that can be incorporated into warm-up routines. This works well for new hymns, songs, or even psalm tones included on the rehearsal docket.

The questions, ideas, and techniques mentioned so far are appropriate for choirs of all ages, especially children. Too often, our culture demands that we make things simpler for children, and excruciatingly so. For the church this often results in music that is repetitive and trite, more about cutesiness than about proclamation, praise, or prayer. Children understand much more than we tend to assume. For that matter, so do our assemblies. In the fourth century, Basil the Great wrote that "those who are children in actual age" as well as the young at heart seldom leave worship "easily retaining in memory some maxim of either the Apostles or the Prophets, but they do sing the texts of the psalms at home and circulate them in the marketplace."[7] In Basil's time, children bore great responsibility for the proclamation of the word. Early uses of the word *lector* were, in some places, associated with children, particularly boys whose families wanted them to develop skills in rhetoric and oratory necessary for careers in civic service. Writers of the time acknowledged that youths would grow into their understanding of a text, even if all the words did not make sense at first. Today, regardless of age, all of us continue to grow into our understanding of texts in our Bibles and hymnals; there is no reason to stifle young imaginations with diluted versions of scripture, songs, or sermons, nor is there any reason children should be kept from serving as readers, greeters, musicians, or members of the procession.

The early church understood the benefits of entrusting youth with significant responsibility, an integral role rooted in scripture rather than simplistic reduction "at their level." While teaching strategies may be age-appropriate in design, content does not have to be filtered or stripped of meaning. A children's choir that regularly sings hymn stanzas in worship is ultimately more beneficial and lasting than a seasonal pageant to be applauded at. Nor does music for children need to be simplified

7   Basil the Great, "Homilia in psalmum," trans. James McKinnon in *Music in Early Christian Literature* (Cambridge and New York: Cambridge University Press, 1987), 65.

to the extent that it is bland or merely entertaining—what Carl Schalk calls a diet of musical "junk food"! Rather, let children sing the same hymns as their parents, siblings, and grandparents around eucharistic tables in worship and around meal tables in homes. In similar fashion, young instrumentalists can develop technical skills through the practice of hymns; both melodies and descants provide exercises in learning about key signatures, scales, rhythms, intonation, and more. Let hymnals be the songbooks used in Sunday school and vacation Bible school offerings. Let these words and melodies take hold in young imaginations. We have much to learn from the young among us: let their wisdom and insight teach us too!

Cantors and staff colleagues

In addition to cultivating trusting relationships with their assemblies and fellow musicians, cantors endeavor to establish honest and respectful partnerships with staff colleagues such as pastors, deacons, lay staff, administrators, teachers, sextons, volunteers, and all who offer their gifts of time and talent as part of their respective vocations. Healthy partnerships are founded upon mutual trust, and trust is both rooted in and strengthened by clear, direct communication. For example:

- Cantors should consult fellow staff members when planning activities in the worship space such as practice, lessons, instrument maintenance, rehearsals, and the like (a shared Google Calendar or similar tool is useful for this).
- Check with the administrative assistant or office volunteers

before beginning a large copying project, just to make sure they hadn't planned to print and fold worship folders earlier than usual for some reason.

- Discuss practice times with the sexton: even though you may not mind the work of the sexton or maintenance crew in the worship space, they may mind your practicing.
- A lay leader who schedules acolytes, readers, and communion servers may find it helpful to have a copy of the choir roster and schedule so as to avoid schedule conflicts.
- Rather than engaging in stealth thermostat conflicts—one person dials the temperature up, another dials it down—cantors should take care to educate colleagues about the optimal temperature and humidity conditions for church instruments.

Staff members should know something about one another's working methods and communication preferences, and discuss what is most appropriate for everyone's needs. A musician who prefers to work in the early morning and correspond by email may find it frustrating that the pastor sends text messages in the evening hours. Some find it helpful to be copied on every email message or conversation thread; some find that unhelpful, perhaps overwhelming. Open, honest, and thoughtful communication—striving to see beyond one's specific area or responsibility—helps us honor the vocations of our colleagues. Ministry, musical or otherwise, does not happen in a vacuum.

Perhaps the most important relationships that cantors cultivate are those with pastors. In most cases, these are the two roles that bear primary responsibility for worship and worship planning. In her book *Rivals or a Team? Clergy-Musician Relationships in the Twenty-First Century*, Eileen Guenther lists qualities shared by pastors and musicians that can help foster a sense of partnership instead of competition. She notes that both pastors and musicians: are highly intuitive and motivated, share a sense of call, share nurturing and pastoral qualities, tend to avoid conflict and please others, are usually under-compensated, and are publicly evaluated on a weekly basis.[8] An effective pastor-musician team is not only based on shared values and a shared sense of vocation, but also on honest communication. Both should be willing and able to acknowledge their concerns—personal and professional—with one another, to be assured that they can ask for help or guidance when needed. Like any relationship, an effective partnership arises from a sense of humility, not guarding one's turf or surreptitiously working to advance a personal agenda. As N. Lee Orr has written:

> Together, the minister and musician must each leave their fiefdoms of pulpit and choir loft and forge a partnership. For the pastor, this means stepping down from the lofty realms of being the CEO and standing on common ground with the musician, the rest of the staff, and the congregation. It also means that the musician must leave the secure

8   Eileen Morris Guenther, *Rivals or a Team? Clergy-Musician Relationships in the Twenty-First Century* (St. Louis: MorningStar Music Publishers, 2012), 15–17.

artistic shelter behind the altar rail [or balcony]
and join the entire church community—clergy
and congregation—in worshiping together.[9]

Unfortunately, the separate training programs for musicians and pastors have largely neglected to teach or even discuss these important skills. Accordingly, pastors and musicians must take it upon themselves to figure out what works best for their personalities, staff dynamics, changing contexts, and assemblies. In your setting, what might it look like if the pastor and musician decide to:

- Lead a lectionary study together?
- Attend synod assemblies or conferences together?
- Discuss books or articles from worship resources together?
- Discuss self-care with one another?

More practically, and as with their partnerships with other staff colleagues, pastors and musicians can help one another by discussing aspects of their working relationships such as days off, usual working hours (especially for part-time and volunteer musicians), optimal times to "debrief" recent worship services, and preferred communication methods. They should also discuss best practices for potentially difficult situations such as attempts at triangulation by a third party—when pastoral concerns are brought to the musician by a member of the

---

9   N. Lee Orr, *The Church Music Handbook for Pastors and Musicians* (Nashville: Abingdon Press, 1991), 47.

choir, when complaints about the musician are expressed to the pastor, or when approached by council or vestry members about financial matters that affect the community. Pastors and musicians should together realize that conflict is not a prospective *if* but an eventual *when* and work to develop partnerships based on understanding, perspective, affirmation, and trust—all of which are essential for negotiating conflict in ways that honor their shared concern for the assembly's worship.

Finally, cantors may wish to cultivate a network of colleagues beyond their immediate contexts—perhaps a local cantor or easily reachable friend elsewhere—with whom they can discuss problematic situations openly and in strict confidence. Colleagues and friends not only provide a listening ear, but often supply clarity, advice, and, if necessary, an unvarnished assessment about how a cantor's actions may have caused or inflamed conflict. Venting or ranting on public forums such as Facebook or to members of the choir about siblings in Christ (or even resources that represent the faithful work of God's people) is not only unprofessional but stands in opposition to the eighth commandment. As Luther reminds us in the *Large Catechism*, "We should use our tongue to speak only the best about all people" and honor their vocations. "Our chief reason for doing this," Luther explains, "is the one that Christ has given in the gospel, and in which he means to encompass all the commandments concerning our neighbor, 'In everything do to others as you would have them do to you.'"[10]

---

10   Robert Kolb and Timothy J. Wengert, eds., *The Book of Concord: The Confessions of the Evangelical Lutheran Church* (Minneapolis: Fortress Press, 2000), 424.

Cantors and culture

This book has frequently mentioned the role of context in shaping the vocations of church musicians and the assemblies they serve. Local contexts, however, are part of wider cultures, their threads tangled together in a dense web of interlocking networks and relationships. Accordingly, the church's musical expressions are simultaneously *constructs* that, in one direction, reflect culture and *constructors* that, in the opposite direction, shape culture.[11] So, to conclude this chapter, a few observations about culture and church musicians.

Having marked the 500th anniversary of the Reformation in 2017, we now stand at the threshold of the third decade of the twenty-first century. This is both an exciting and a difficult time to be a church musician. On the one hand, we are blessed with an abundance of resources: the manifold gifts of the Spirit are poured out in new texts and new melodies that can be transmitted instantaneously around the globe. A musician in the rural Midwest can watch YouTube videos of African drumming in order to lead songs from the African continent in ways that honor indigenous tradition and practice. There is so much stuff, and so much access—daunting to sift through, but nonetheless exhilarating. How can we possibly keep from singing? On the other hand, this abundance of possibility is terrifying in its demands for at least basic familiarity, let alone expertise. Many cantors feel pressured to attain fluency in the styles and instrumental

11   T. David Gordon, *Why Johnny Can't Sing Hymns: How Pop Culture Rewrote the Hymnal* (Phillipsburg, NJ: P & R Publications, 2010), 1.

techniques needed to lead (or facilitate leadership of) the panoply of hymns, songs, and other musical expressions available at our fingertips. *Evangelical Lutheran Worship* alone—not counting myriad other resources—includes plainsong melodies first sung more than a thousand years ago alongside praise choruses that are just a few decades old, not to mention everything in between. For some, demands made by new resources could not have been envisioned as part of their training. Thankfully, organizations such as the Association of Lutheran Church Musicians provide forums for learning and practicing new skills through conferences, workshops, webinars, and the like. As mentioned in the following chapter, church musicians deserve both the encouragement and support, financial or otherwise, to pursue opportunities for continuing education.

Together, we—musicians, pastors, the church—should acknowledge that the twenty-first-century church musician is situated in a culture in which music is widely viewed as an entertainment to be consumed, not a communal activity. Technology has equipped us with the ability to surround ourselves with customized playlists of music we like, to exist in echo chambers with those who share our narrow opinions, to revel in our individualism and materialism. Unfortunately, many of these consumerist tendencies—not to mention the corporate and hierarchical models advanced by megachurches—have unduly influenced our approach to worship, dividing communities according to their musical preferences or demographic identities. At the same time, many communities lament declining attendance and diminishing choirs. Spaces built for large assemblies now feel empty. Reflecting cultural attitudes toward music, musicians are often called to turn these trends around—immediately. Musical style is often (incorrectly) seen as a magical elixir: a new style, a new service, a new everything will be the cure and remedy for this grief. The increasing absence of sound musical and liturgical training in our seminaries and lack of theological training for musicians has only compounded these cultural challenges.

Our time and place demand flexibility, just as in earlier centuries. Recall, for instance, how Heinrich Schütz adapted his compositional style in response to the Thirty Years' War, especially to financial hardships and the absence of singers called away to military service. And recall how Bach repurposed his music, revising cantatas and passions throughout his career. But flexibility is harder for us today because we are trained to think in nineteenth-century terms—of fixed scores issued by publishers for the musical marketplace, of perfected performances by virtuosos, of great composers issuing masterworks for posterity. We have been conditioned to respond rather than create, to consume music in its edited, stereophonic perfection rather than encourage voices who seek to praise the Lord with a joyful noise. To counter consumerist tendencies, we do well to consider ways in which musical power can be broken so as to empower our assemblies, to journey through the rich treasury of Spirit-inspired art and music in a manner faithful to the gospel of Christ rather than the gospel of culture.

Thus, an important aspect of the cantor's work in today's culture is to foster awareness of cultural assumptions that stand in the way of assembly singing. This will bring both joy and discomfort, affirmation and criticism. To give sustained attention to context and community—their complexity, richness, and messiness—is a daunting task, but if we can reorient ourselves away from market forces and back toward our contexts and people, perhaps we can attain a measure of clarity about what matters most for our respective communities. This does not mean bowing to every contextual or cultural demand: we need to sing honestly of topics such as death—not of "passing away," of "ending a life journey," nor any of the quaint euphemisms that unsuccessfully mask its reality. The tugs and pulls that stem from our attention to context and culture help form a taut and sturdy center, one capable of supporting the combined gravitas of all we can pour into it. As Mark Bangert has observed, "The responsible leader in the church's worship will strive to get congregants to repeat week by week what will be true and helpful for a lifetime."[12] In all contexts and circumstances, may the work of cantors in their communities model the hospitality, welcome, and fellowship shared at the Lord's table:

---

12 Mark P. Bangert, "Rehabilitating the Vocation of Cantor with the Help of the Early Church and Johannes Bugenhagen," in *Subject to None, Servant of All: Essays in Christian Scholarship in Honor of Kurt Karl Hendel*, ed. Peter Vethanayagamony and Kenneth Sawyer (Minneapolis: Lutheran University Press, 2016), 86.

> Give us grace to live for others,
> serving all, both friends and strangers,
> seeking justice, love, and mercy
> till you come in final glory.[13]

13   Joel W. Lundeen, "Now we join in celebration," in *Evangelical Lutheran Worship*, #462. Text
     © Joel W. Lundeen, admin. Augsburg Fortress.

Resources

Books

- Girlinghouse, Michael K. *Embracing God's Future without Forgetting the Past: A Conversation about Loss, Grief, and Nostalgia in Congregational Life.* Minneapolis: Fortress Press, 2019.
- Highben, Zebulon M., and Kristina M. Langlois, eds. *With a Voice of Singing: Essays on Children, Choirs, and Music in the Church in Honor of Ronald A. Nelson.* Minneapolis: Kirk House Publishers, 2007.
- Miller, Barbara Day. *Encounters with the Holy: A Conversational Model for Worship Planning.* Herndon, VA: Alban Institute, 2010.
- Mueller, Craig. *Any Body There? Worship and Being Human in a Digital Age.* Eugene, OR: Wipf & Stock, 2017.
- Quivik, Melinda A., Suzanne K. Burke, Martin A. Seltz, and Julie O'Brien, eds. *Leading Worship Matters: A Sourcebook for Preparing Worship Leaders.* Minneapolis: Augsburg Fortress, 2013.
- Raabe, Nancy. *One-Minute Devotions for the Church Musician,* 3 vols. St. Louis: MorningStar Music Publishers, 2010–2012 (volumes correspond to cycles A, B, and C of the Revised Common Lectionary).
- Willetts, Sandra. *Beyond the Downbeat: Choral Rehearsal Skills and Techniques.* Nashville: Abingdon Press, 2000.

Articles and chapters

- Baxter, Andrea. "The Integrative Approach to Children in Worship." *CrossAccent: Journal of the Association of Lutheran Church Musicians* 20.1 (March 2012): 19–25.
- Bouman, Walter R. "Partners in Proclamation: Pastors and Musicians, A Theologian's Perspective." *CrossAccent: Journal of the Association of Lutheran Church Musicians* 14.3 (2006): 5–12.
- Fothergill, Chad. "'Peel Here': Labels and Language in Worship Planning." *CrossAccent: Journal of the Association of Lutheran Church Musicians* 23.2 (Summer 2015): 18–26.
- Fothergill, Chad. "Silence and Song: Attending to the Full Voice of the Assembly." *CrossAccent: Journal of the Association of Lutheran Church Musicians* 24.1 (Spring 2016): 35–43.
- Quivik, Melinda A. "Written and Sung into the Hungry Body." *CrossAccent: Journal of the Association of Lutheran Church Musicians* 20.1 (March 2012): 6–13.
- Senn, Frank C. "History and Culture." In *Introduction to Christian Liturgy*, 17–41. Minneapolis: Fortress Press, 2012.
- Westermeyer, Paul. "Discernment." *CrossAccent: Journal of the Association of Lutheran Church Musicians* 19.1 (2011): 5–16.

Calling a cantor

The final chapter of this book, primarily intended for pastors and others tasked with hiring church musicians, may also be useful to musicians contemplating a new position—and perhaps even for musicians whose positions are in the midst of change. Irrespective of role, all involved should bear in mind that transitions in congregational leadership are accompanied by a wide range of individual and collective emotions: celebration of a faithful ministry, thanksgiving for the gift of friendship, grief at leavetaking, and sometimes sorrow and anger. Regardless of cause, transitions in musical leadership provide opportunity for a community to assess—with appropriate sensitivity and pastoral care due the moment—its needs, gifts, abilities, and mission with respect to the singing assembly that gathers for worship. Accordingly, the selection of a new cantor should never be taken lightly, nor should it fall to a select few to make a swift decision on behalf of the entire community. Rather, the process of inviting a new cantor—either during an interim period or once a departure has been announced—should have both breadth and depth in the community.

Discerning "wants" and "needs"

While it may be easy to catalog the responsibilities of the incumbent cantor and then post that list as the job description, such procedures are often short-sighted and can easily lead to conflict, especially when newcomers are expected to function as clones of their predecessors without regard for their own gifts, personalities, and working styles. Rather, the selection of a new cantor should emerge from a variety of conversations over a period of time. Perhaps some will involve the entire community in an adult forum; perhaps others will only involve the choir, worship committee, or staff; perhaps others will only occur between the search committee and a designated consultant. Though interrelated, many of these conversations revolve around key questions such as these:

- Is the community searching for a vocationally oriented "church musician" or an occupationally oriented "musician who happens to serve in a church"?
- In what ways are financial considerations shaping the conversation? What distinctions are being made between a "bottom line" and an "investment" in the congregation's life?
- Is the community aware that a search committee has been established? Have non-committee members been given opportunity to express their visions too? Does this conversation have the sense of being lifted from the community or imposed upon it?
- Is the pastor searching for a "yes" person who will acquiesce to autocratic decisions or for a colleague who will

engage in meaningful conversation about liturgy, music, and formation?

- Are conversations about liturgy and music framed in terms of spiritual formation and nourishment instead of attendance statistics and stylistic popularity?
- Will the position description allow a particular candidate's gifts to live, move, and grow into and within the position?
- Have the musician's "unseen" tasks—such as lectionary study for hymn selection, the composition of a psalm setting or descant for a beginning instrumentalist, the preparation and practice of assembly song, score study and rehearsal planning, or reading professional journals—been accounted in determining the hours per week allotted for the position?
- Has time been provided for the cantor's self-care?
- Are there opportunities for the cantor to further her craft by attending services at other congregations, or through periodic sabbaticals?

A community will also want to articulate some of its most important needs as it considers the type of musician best suited to lead its singing. Church musicians possess a wide array of abilities. Some skills are established primarily through training, others through experience. Depending on the size and scope of the position, a community may wish to identify the primary attributes it seeks in a cantor, such as the following:

- A **leader** who works well with all other ministries in the community
- A **child of God** who sees the community as fellow children of God

- A **pastoral presence** who can thoughtfully guide conversations about changing styles and demographics
- A **planner** who is attentive to the arc of Sundays, seasons, and community life
- A **conductor** or **administrator** who can effectively plan for and lead a variety of groups in rehearsal and in worship
- An **accompanist** who is technically proficient in one or more instruments
- A **teacher** capable of balancing inherited wisdom with new ideas
- A **student** who seeks to improve, learn, and develop a deeper understanding of the community and its musical expressions
- A **designer** of materials that assist the worship life of the assembly such as worship folders, projected material, or new musical compositions
- A **colleague** in the wider community of professional musicians
- A **steward** of property, equipment, and financial resources

Though all of these are desirable attributes, different communities have different needs. One assembly may need a teacher more than a composer, while another may need a pastorally inclined musician who delights in leading assembly song from an aging organ more than a seasoned performer accustomed to playing dazzling recitals in large, reverberant cathedrals. Often, personal qualities matter more than professional skills. Cantors who see Christ in all of God's children and who joyfully lead the assembly to the best of their ability are—despite arthritic hands or failing eyesight—more likely to inspire the assembly singing than professional musicians who demand perfection and continually voice their dissatisfaction with whatever they perceive as substandard.

> Prioritizing the community's needs makes for a better job description, a better interview, a better match, and better assembly singing—indeed, a more profound "alleluia"!

A community will also need to consider whether the musician should be offered a letter of agreement (contract) or letter of call. For musicians who are rostered as Ministers of Word and Sacrament or Ministers of Word and Service, a letter of call is most appropriate. However, it is helpful to understand that all church musicians are, in essence, called to their positions—if not by the congregation, then by the Holy Spirit. Recognizing the communal nature of music making, some musicians are hired or called by congregations (usually through a church council, vestry, or executive committee) rather than by a pastor or senior pastor. Such an arrangement ensures that the musician's work is oriented toward the assembly and not dependent upon a single personality or hierarchical bureaucracy.

Crafting a position description

After conversations about the community's needs, it will be necessary to write a position description, ideally a document that is grounded in mission and invites possibility rather than a prescribed list of bullet points. Too often, position descriptions for musicians begin with organizational structure—"reports to" so and so—and proceed with lengthy, unorganized lists of requirements, goals, and dreams. None of those ingredients are bad, but in the wrong order they can be a recipe for disappointment. Rather, a description ideally begins with language that welcomes and honors a potential applicant's sense of call and vocation along with clear statements regarding hours per week, salary, desired start date, and whether or not benefits can be expected. A hypothetical example:

> As leader of the people's song, the cantor at *congregation name* serves both as minister and musician in the local community, the wider church, and the world that Christ has commanded us to love and serve. All that the cantor does should be grounded in a clear understanding of word and sacrament. Other ministries, activities, and programs in our congregation receive their meaning from an understanding of worship as the central activity of this faith community. As a leader and teacher, the cantor works to equip others with tools for building and sharing their faith through God's gift of music. This is a salaried position (up to $47,500 per year) without benefits averaging between 20–25 hours per week. A start date in the late spring or early summer is desired.

And, for good measure, an actual example:

> *Name* Lutheran Church is a well-rooted and renewing congregation in *location*. Scandinavian in its heritage, it

is passionate about creating a wide welcome in worship and seeking justice in society for marginalized people. Though small in number, the congregation has a strong voice in the community. This voice connects to regular worship, where folks from many walks of life find worth, meaning, mercy, and relationship. We are a committed Reconciling in Christ church, which means we welcome and involve LGBTQIA+ persons at all levels of community life. The church's song plays a big role in that welcome. We seek a Director of Music who will help us cultivate our deep neighborhood roots and wide outward reach.

Then, by way of continued introduction, perhaps describe key features of the community for potential applicants:

Ours is an urban congregation of 750 members that strives to fulfill its mission of being "called to hope in Christ." Our proximity to a large university allows for an active campus ministry and exploration of musical styles served by the gifts of students who participate in the choir and as instrumentalists. We serve a weekly meal to those in need, and attendance by residents of our surrounding neighborhoods has enriched our singing through the addition of many Latin American and African American musical styles. Public transit allows easy access to other parts of the city, as well as to major metropolitan areas nearby.

Search committees should also prepare materials that address practical concerns of applicants such as information about local school districts or other musical opportunities that can supplement part-time work. Pertinent details about the position's specific requirements and responsibilities can follow in clearly organized categories and supporting statements. For example:

Leading assembly song

- Summary of activities as principal musician—keyboardist, conductor, composer, or combinations thereof—for all regular and festival liturgies, midweek services during Advent and Lent
- Instruction to arrange for qualified and capable substitutes when absent for personal or professional reasons
- Expectations such as "first right of refusal" for occasional services including weddings and funerals (and how the musician is compensated for these)

Teaching and learning

- Responsibilities regarding musical instruction for children
- Possibilities regarding other educational offerings in the congregation through newsletter articles, adult forum presentations, or other media
- Opportunities and expectations for personal and professional growth through organizational memberships or attendance at workshops and conferences such as those offered by the Association of Lutheran Church Musicians or the Hymn Society (noting whether or not attendance at professional gatherings will be counted toward personal vacation)

Administration and planning

- Role in liturgical planning such as the selection of hymnody, liturgical settings, and other music
- Responsibility for proper maintenance of all musical instruments of the church by qualified persons, securing proper copyrights and permissions, and stewardship of other material resources such as the music library
- Description of responsibilities related to budget and participation in worship-related committees

In the congregation and community

- Invitation to use the church's instruments for private musical instruction
- Expectations about scheduling and advertising concerts or other events related to worship and music
- Description of ways the congregation supports the cantor such as paying for substitutes when the cantor is away, maintaining written guidance for weddings and funerals, and providing channels for resolution of potential conflicts

Qualifications

- Bearing in mind that advanced degrees in performance are not always indicators of the ability to effectively lead assembly song, what gifts and previous experience best describe the needs of the community?
- Other than musical proficiencies, what other skills—such as working with youth, working with a large staff, or familiarity with specialized software for engraving or worship-folder design—will be useful?

Compensation and benefits

- What should potential applicants know about benefits such as insurance, continuing education, vacation, parental leave, or sabbaticals?

Reporting and evaluation

- Identification of direct supervisor(s) and expectations regarding reviews and evaluation such as these excerpts from actual position descriptions:

"The cantor is accountable, first of all, to the Lord of the Church for her or his ministry. In the setting of this parish the cantor is responsible to the pastor for the performance of specific duties and responsibilities. This position description is reviewed each year by the cantor, the pastor, and the Mutual Ministry Committee."

"The Cantor serves under the supervision of the Parish Pastor and the Campus Pastor and is responsible to the Congregational Council. A performance evaluation will be administered annually by the Personnel Committee with input from the Congregational Council."

A position description might also include specific details about instruments and equipment as well as noting logistical challenges presented by their configuration. This is especially important for musicians expected to conduct or accompany choirs from mechanical-action organ consoles attached to their cases, an arrangement that sometimes results in the choir being positioned behind rather than in front of the organist.

Finally, the position description can conclude with a list of materials that applicants are expected to submit, such as a cover letter, résumé or curriculum vitae, repertoire list, names and contact information for references, or links to audiovisual material, if desired. If appropriate, the description can conclude with an approximate timeline for the remainder of the search process such as a date when review of applications begins (or a date when applications will no longer be considered).

The search process

Once a position description has been drafted, reviewed, edited, and revised, it can be distributed through local, regional, and national organizations that provide job-listing services, including:

- Association of Lutheran Church Musicians:
  https://alcm.org/job-listings/
- Synod offices such as:
  http://mpls-synod.org/for-congregations/job-opportunities/worship-and-music-lay-job-opportunities/
- Institute of Sacred Music (Yale University):
  https://ism.yale.edu/job-listings
- American Choral Directors Association:
  https://www.careerwebsite.com/?site_id=18712
- American Guild of Organists: https://jobs.agohq.org/
  (many local chapters also maintain lists of open positions)

- Choristers Guild: https://www.choristersguild.org/4DCGI/jobbank/index.html
- Handbell Musicians of America: http://handbellmusicians.org/events-networking/handbellexchange/

It may also be worthwhile to establish connections with worship-related faculty at institutions such as:

- ELCA colleges and universities: https://www.elca.org/Our-Work/Leadership/Colleges-and-Universities
- ELCA seminaries: https://elcaseminaries.org
- Degree programs in organ, some of which include sacred music studies: https://www.agohq.org/academic-degree-programs/

Position descriptions can also travel far and wide through Facebook postings, as well as through networks of friends and colleagues.

Communication between applicants and search committees should strive for clarity and hospitality. Each applicant should receive an acknowledgment that, in addition to confirming receipt of materials, provides an approximate timeline for appropriate stages of the search process such as phone or video interviews, the contacting of references, and on-site auditions. For candidates invited to audition, committees should be prepared to field questions about travel reimbursement, accommodations, and practice time. Applicants who are no longer under consideration should be notified as soon as possible. Above all, they should be thanked for their interest in the position, for time invested in preparing application materials, and for their continued ministry. A personalized message—as simple as the salutation "Dear *name*"—is always more appropriate than a generic and impersonal email. Any applicant interviewed by the committee should receive subsequent updates about the search process through a telephone call. These are the marks of courtesy and professionalism, the same gracious hospitality shown at the eucharistic table where all are welcomed and fed.

Committees will also want to carefully plan their interview and audition procedures. Though each context is different, interviews and auditions should reveal understanding of the candidate's sense of vocation and vision; ability to lead assembly song in styles appropriate to the instruments, spaces, and community; and compatibility with other requirements of the role. Depending on the size and scope of the position, auditions can include leading assembly song (for the committee, the choir, and perhaps even the full assembly on a Sunday morning), rehearsal, and other requisite tasks. Often, it is helpful for candidates to demonstrate their familiarity with several styles and techniques through an array of hymns and songs. Committees may do well to suggest scenarios such as "introduce and lead the hymn of the day for Easter Sunday" or "lead a quieter hymn for evening prayer" or "introduce and lead a new, unfamiliar hymn." An audition weighted toward the performance of repertoire (as if playing a recital) along with a couple of indiscriminate hymn stanzas does little to show how an applicant will love, serve, and nurture the voice of the assembly that gathers for worship.

Finally, make plans to affirm the new cantor's vocation and ministry in the context of worship through rites such as Installation of Lay Professional Staff in *Evangelical Lutheran Worship: Occasional Services for the Assembly* (p. 101) or the Affirmation of Christian Vocation in *Evangelical Lutheran Worship* (p. 84). Welcome them in the name of Christ, welcome their call, and honor their service in the assembly and their witness to the world.

Resources

Books

- Bradley, C. Randall. *From Postlude to Prelude: Music Ministry's Other Six Days*. Rev. ed. St. Louis: MorningStar Music Publishers, 2015.
- Long, Kimberly. *The Worshipping Body: The Art of Leading Worship*. Louisville, KY: Westminster John Knox Press, 2009.
- Roberts, William Bradley. *Music and Vital Congregations: A Practical Guide for Clergy*. New York: Church Publishing, 2009.
- Satterlee, Craig A. *When God Speaks through Worship: Stories Congregations Live By*. Herndon, VA: Alban Institute, 2009.
- Wells, Samuel. *Incarnational Ministry: Being with the Church*. Grand Rapids, MI: William B. Eerdmans, 2017.
- Westermeyer, Paul. *A High and Holy Calling: Essays of Encouragement for the Church and Its Musicians*. St. Louis: MorningStar Music Publishers, 2018.
- Westermeyer, Paul. *The Church Musician*. Rev. ed. Minneapolis: Augsburg Fortress, 1997.

Website

- Association of Lutheran Church Musicians, "Guidelines for the Employment of Musicians in the Lutheran Church," https://alcm.org/wp-content/uploads/2012/06/Placement-Employment-Guidelines-2017.pdf.

In all places and forever
glory be expressed
to the Son, with God the Father
and the Spirit blest:
in our worship and our living
keep us striving for the best.

"Come to us, creative Spirit"
Evangelical Lutheran Worship #687

Postlude

Recall the four musicians introduced in this book's prelude, each preparing to lead the singing of their assemblies on that Sunday in January, the festival of the Baptism of Our Lord. Beneath the sonic variety of their songs and musical expressions are their experiences and stories of planning, collaboration, practice, teaching, discernment, joys, and frustrations—all different, but all united by a common vocation: to serve and attend to their assemblies through God's gift of music, to sing the living voice of the gospel.

To be a church musician, to live into this high and holy calling, is to immerse oneself in the familiar, yet bend toward the countercultural, radical, and prophetic. To sing welcome in the face of discrimination. To sing peace in the face of violence and war. To proclaim God's justice despite our desires and wants. As Paul reminds us in his letter to the Ephesians, God's unbounded mercy and love "made us alive together with Christ" (Eph. 2:4-5). Church musicians see and hear diverse voices of the full body of Christ, voices that speak at once from generations past, from faraway lands, from down the street, from the here and now.

Assembly song invites us to remember the long arc of our story—a pilgrim people, not an institutional church. Each time the assembly gathers, we are invited to wash ourselves in the waters of God's grace poured out in the rich treasury of song. This song began before us, and it will continue after us. But here, in this time and place, we—pastors and cantors alike—are called to faithfully tend and nurture that song and the voice of all God's people who sing it.

And so, we pray:

> O God of majesty, whom saints and angels delight to worship: Pour out your Spirit on your servants who, with the gifts of music, enliven our praises and proclaim your word with power. Through this ministry give us new awareness of your beauty and grace, and join our voices with all the choirs of heaven, both now and forever; through your Son, Jesus Christ, our Lord. Amen. (*ELW*, p. 74)